PUTTING THE OUTSIDE INSIDE KIDS

A Father's Algonquin Journey
With His Daughter

Bill Kennedy

Putting the Outside Inside Kids
Copyright © 2018 by Bill Kennedy

No part of this publication may be reproduced, distributed, or transmitted in any form or by any means, including photocopying, recording, or other electronic or mechanical methods, without the prior written permission of the author, except in the case of brief quotations embodied in critical reviews and certain other non-commercial uses permitted by copyright law.

camping, canoeing, children, nature, philosophy, wilderness

Tellwell Talent
www.tellwell.ca

ISBN
978-1-77370-634-4 (Hardcover)
978-1-77370-633-7 (Paperback)
978-1-77370-635-1 (eBook)

For my wife, Bev; my daughters, Suzanne and Laurie; my grandchildren, Brian, Kelsey, Ben, Emily and Scott; and my son-in-law, Simon — fellow paddlers all in that paradise called Algonquin Park.

*In those vernal seasons of the year
when the air is calm and pleasant,
it were an injury and sullenness
against nature not to go out and see
her riches and partake in her
rejoicing with heaven and earth.*
- John Milton

Preface

The butterscotch pudding tin sits on the bookshelf in front of me as I write this. The size of a teacup and riddled with holes from the incisors of a marauding black bear, it has been a prized possession of mine for more than half my life. The pudding is long gone, of course, but the tin remains full to overflowing with the images of that sunlit blue and green wilderness from a long-ago canoeing adventure I took with my daughter when she was five years old.

Thinking back through all the intervening years, it is the memories of the great outdoors I share with my children and grandchildren that rise like cream to the top. They are the signposts along a mental map I can retrace anytime I want, from our camping trips through the Maritimes and Ontario to the prairies, the Yukon and wild Pacific shore. In the heady aroma of damp earth and cedar along a forest trail or in the sharp air of ice and pine on a Rocky Mountain pass, they dance a fiddler's jig, bittersweet, treasured and irreplaceable beyond measure. A love for nature is a gift from me to my children and from them to their children, a bond for generations of our family.

The importance of the link between man and nature has been a theme for writers since antiquity. Two millennia ago, the Roman satirist Juvenal recognized this when he wrote that never does nature say one thing and wisdom another. Regrettably, we have barely listened and the earth is suffering the consequences. As parents, we all can help by giving our children the gift of nature and thereby fostering inquiry into the health of this planet that struggles to sustain us. In this country of Canada, nature is a gift never far from hand. Young children are imagination in action. They respond to the outdoors like ducks to water. A seed hidden in the heart of an apple, so goes the Welsh proverb, is an orchard invisible. If we do the weeding and watering, the flowers will blossom.

Early one morning not so long ago, a man and a boy, presumably father and son, sat down across from me at a coffee shop near my home. The boy was six or seven years old, freckled, his thatch of brown hair sticking out in all directions. He sat hunched over, his chin just above the tabletop, nibbling around the edge of the muffin he held in both hands. Every once in a while, he would glance up at his father, but his father was in another world and paid him no attention, focused as he was on the glowing palm-sized screen he'd pulled from his pocket. Not once did he acknowledge his son and not once did the little boy say a word.

Paddling quiet lakes and sleeping in the woods and cooking meals over a smoky campfire take us back to a time when our lives were lived in daily communion with the earth, and family, not technology, was the heart of our reality. We need to keep a place for that connection. "In wildness," wrote Henry David Thoreau, "is the preservation of the world."

A Few Words from Suzanne

I was five years old when my father and I made the Algonquin Park canoe trip described in this book. So it's hard for me to say how much of that trip I actually remember and how much of it is remembrance through hearing stories retold and watching the movie film that recorded it. But I can say with certainty that some of my earliest memories are of our family's annual camping trips that took us across the country.

When I hear the word *nature,* the first image I see is a blend of all those campsites I've been to through the years. The second image I see is that of my father. Happiest in the outdoors and canoeing on pristine lakes, he encouraged my sister and me to get involved in outdoor activities at an early age. Playing at the campgrounds or on the beach, riding a lake's high waves on an air mattress with my mother, and sitting around the campfire at night, telling stories or jokes and roasting marshmallows, remain a vivid part of my childhood. To this day, the smell of wood smoke takes me back instantly to those earlier times.

Nowadays, in my career as a schoolteacher, I work in cities around the world and try to adapt my outdoor experiences to city environments. A bug crossing the floor in my classroom is more likely to become a science lesson and an example of compassion for all living things rather than something to squash underfoot. In Shenzhen, China, there are huge plantings of flowers and trees along roads and highways. On my way to work, I always looked to see how they were blooming, which ones needed water or which ones might have been damaged by the latest typhoon. The lilac and magnolia blossoms in Kiev, Ukraine, dressed that post-Soviet-era city in one of the most glorious springtimes I've seen. Finding nature in the swirl of foreign city life makes it a more welcoming place for me.

I could not agree more with the idea expressed in this book — that many of the lessons nature instills in us as children remain, if not overtly, certainly in our subconscious. Regrettably, it has been my observation that knowledge of the natural world is not something I've readily found in my students. It is minimal at best. The encouraging observation, however, is the enthusiasm they show in learning about nature when given the opportunity, especially children in the early grades.

Life in the outdoors, I believe, has made me more resilient. Nature doesn't mollycoddle. No wailing when you trip and fall over a tree root, just pick yourself up and carry on. The lake is icy cold, go swimming or not. Raining! That's what rain gear is for. Mosquitos? Here's the insect repellant. Growing up camping and canoeing and hiking in the woods are part of who I am, and I'm thankful my parents gave me that experience.

- Suzanne Kennedy

Suzanne canoeing on the Salmon River near Roblin, Ontario, 2017.

N

Little Otterslide

Caroline Island

Burnt Island

Tom Thomson

Littledoe

Baby Joe

Little Joe

Tepee

Joe Island

Joe

Tom Thomson Cairn

Cook Island
Canoe Lake

HWY 60

The lakes on our Algonquin Park canoe trip

Scale: 1 inch to 2 miles

Map drawn from "The Friends of Algonquin Park" canoe route map.

1

*And Nature, the old nurse, took
The child upon her knee,
Saying: "Here is a story-book
Thy Father has written for thee."*
– Henry Wadsworth Longfellow

"Come on, Dad. Let's go."

Suzanne stood with her back to the lake, her attention focused on the last of her ice cream cone, not looking at me as she spoke, her mouth smeared with chocolate. I was anxious to go, but the wind with its smell of rain had me thinking again about my plan to shove off right away. Wind and rain. Not choice companions on a canoe trip, especially the wind. It came out of a grey sky from the northwest, herding white-tipped waves in our direction. The French-Canadian voyageurs called it *La Vieille*, the Old Lady, and even those intrepid paddlers were known to languish ashore when she was in a temper on Georgian Bay or Lake Superior. This lake, Canoe Lake, was a major embarkation point for canoe trippers heading into Algonquin Provincial Park's three thousand square miles of wilderness interior. It was no Superior, but neither was I a voyageur.

A gull wheeled low over our heads, its yellow eye searching the ground as it sailed toward the restaurant where other gulls strutted in the busy parking lot, looking for scraps and threatening each other with raucous calls.

"You'd better wash your face."

She dipped her hand in the lake and dabbed her lips.

"Is it warm?" I crouched and let a wave run through my fingers.

"Yep." She wiped the chocolate-coloured water dribbling down her chin onto her shirt sleeve.

The water was pleasantly warm, imparting an unexpected softness. I scooped up a handful of sand and pebbles, grinding them between my palms. Tiny translucent minnows darted just out of reach.

The flotilla of five canoes we had seen far up the lake when we'd first arrived had closed to within a few hundred yards of the beach. The enterprising crews in two of them had joined together by holding onto each other's gunnels and raised a tent fly tied to paddles for a makeshift sail. It billowed in the wind, a huge silver-grey balloon.

It was after eleven o'clock, a late start for us. Ahead lay two hours of paddling, a portage and then more paddling before we would reach the area where I wanted to pitch our first camp. I took off my runners and socks, and pulled our seventy-two-pound blue fibreglass canoe halfway into the water. It had a one-inch-deep keel and a wide beam braced at the centre by a molded portage yoke, and was tough enough not to require the thwarts common to most canoes. In heavy weather its weight was a plus, and as long as I kept the wind in our faces I was sure I could manage. If it forced us left or right and put us broadside to the rolling water, the danger of a capsize could be one miscue away. The power of wind is impressive when it impacts a lone paddler along sixteen feet of hull.

I would sit on the bow seat facing the stern with the heavy canoe pack stowed toward that end as ballast. It was deadweight heavy and would help counterbalance my weight to keep the canoe flat on the water. The pack's design was the equivalent of an oversized canvas potato sack with leather straps and was stuffed with our camping gear and food for the next six days. The smaller clothes pack fit snugly under the stern seat. For now, Suzanne would sit on the floor immediately in front of me where I could reach her in an instant if we ran into trouble. The binoculars, water bottle, map, runners and raincoats went in the space behind me. I looked around. Everything was accounted for, including my copy of the park permit, which identified the lakes where we would camp each night.

Suzanne sat at the water's edge untying her laces. Her little red vinyl pack lay beside her. It contained a few items of clothing along with her Barbie doll and its outfits. She had put her medication in it too, but fearing its loss, I transferred the plastic pill bottle to a small, zippered side pocket on my own pack. I rolled her pants up to her knees.

"Are we going now?"

"Let's wait until the other canoes land."

The canoes hit the beach one after the other, spilling out their passengers in a hubbub of shouts, groans and laughter. They were all girls in their early to middle teens, soaked to the skin, bedraggled, grubby and excited to have found civilization again. They hauled their gear ashore like there was no tomorrow, piled it into a soggy cairn and took off with two of their counsellors in tow for the Portage Store and its restaurant. The third counsellor, and the only male of the group, dragged their green cedarstrip-and-canvas canoes clear of the lake and turned them over to let the water drain. The name Andy was stencilled on the back of his white T-shirt, and on the front was a reproduction of a canoe painting by Frances Anne Hopkins, a nineteenth-century British artist and Canadian resident. Andy was eighteen or nineteen, tall and thin, steel-rimmed glasses. A tension bandage bound his wrist. I asked him about the wind.

It had been no problem for them as it was at their backs all morning. The outbound canoes they had passed seemed to be doing OK too. I felt a little better. And the rain? They had been caught in a heavy downpour right in the middle of packing up this morning and then again out on the lake.

I looked at the sky. It was a mix of overlapping shades of grey sliding over one another at a good clip. Maybe it would blow into a nice afternoon. I spread out the groundsheet over our gear and tucked it down the sides.

"Look! A duck!"

I looked to where Suzanne was pointing. A loon had popped to the surface off to our right very near the shore. It surprised me to see it in an area where there was so much human traffic.

"It's a loon," I said. It wagged its head and in the blink of an eye dove beneath the surface.

"Why does it go under the water?"

"They catch fish to eat. They use their webbed feet like paddles to swim under water and chase fish."

"Can they breathe under the water?"

"No, they can stay under a long time, but they have to come up for air. Look! See? It came up again over there."

The loon had surfaced a little farther up the lake, and far beyond it I could see more canoes. They rode low to the surface, the distance camouflaging their direction of progress. I lay my paddle across the gunnels and jammed the spare one between the canoe pack and the hull.

"OK, let's get your life jacket on."

She held out her arms while I pulled it on and fastened it snugly around her waist. I lifted her into the canoe, instructing her to sit on my life jacket on the floor immediately in front of me.

"I want to sit on the seat."

"Not right now. It's too windy. Maybe later, when it's not so windy."

The wind was not my real concern. She probably would have been fine at the bow. My real concern, though likely unfounded, was the possibility of her experiencing one of her fainting spells or seizures. She had not had one for over a year and a half, and while the medication she was on seemed to be working, I remained wary, and for the time being I wanted her low down on the canoe floor and within arm's reach.

Our two paddles were of the beavertail design and made of ash, a wood that's tough but flexible. There are other designs like the esthetically pleasing otter tail and the longer, slimmer blade of the voyageur paddle, but on the lakes the broader beavertail paddle provides greater thrust for your efforts. Years on, I would switch to the voyageur design, more out of nostalgia for the history of those long-ago days than anything else, and I still use one. I can only guess at the distances it has taken me.

I freed the canoe from the beach and walked it out until there was a half foot of water under the keel. Aiming straight into the wind, I shoved off and hopped in. Suzanne sat with her legs folded under her, gripping the gunnels, her hair blowing from under her red sailor's cap. The tip of my paddle blade caught the crest of a wave as I swung it forward, blowing spray into our faces. Andy hollered after us to have a good trip.

"Can I paddle, Dad?"

"Not just now, OK?" Where she was sitting, it would have been impossible for her to paddle. "The water's pretty rough. Better to wait a bit until we get to where the water's smooth."

I was relieved to find that it was not as tough as I'd expected, although now and then the canoe would rise and smack down. I quickly got it up to twenty-eight strokes a minute and seemed to be keeping on course all right. At the other end of the lake where it split into two narrow arms in the shape of a U, it was bound to be smoother sailing. After that there would be no more wide open water to cross until tomorrow. Hopefully by then the weather would improve.

I hugged the east shore. It combined the advantages of being close to the safety of terra firma along with being the direct route to our campsite destination, and although it did little to abate the buffeting wind, I felt easier. We passed a few cottages, but for the most part the trees came down thickly to the waterline.

A motorboat swept into view, too far away to hear, white spray bursting into the air as it slammed into the waves. Motorboats have a way of making your hard-won efforts in a canoe seem puny, especially on days like this when you're gauging progress one canoe length at a time. I would be glad to get Canoe Lake behind us. Its connection by paved road to Highway 60 made it a popular launch site for motorized watercraft. But once out of Canoe Lake, that should pretty much see the end of them. They are permitted on some of the interior park lakes, but thankfully, after a portage or two, we would rarely see them again.

On our left, Camp Wapomeo, a girls' camp that was founded in 1924, came into view. Inverted canoes lined the dock, a few two-camper sailboats had been hauled ashore near the white lifeguard tower. The tower was a familiar landmark, and when homeward bound it was always the signal that another trip was nearly done.

The peal of the camp bell drifted faintly to us, reminding me of the handbell my teacher had used back when I was in second grade. I glanced at my watch. Twelve fifteen. Maybe the call to lunch. Campers hustled among the green-painted, red-roofed cabins. I was getting a little hungry myself. By one o'clock we'd be at the dam. We could have our lunch then.

Cook Island, a little island just a stone's throw from the mainland, marked the halfway point on the lake, and we hid in its shelter to rest. From here the lake widened with a deep bay on the right. I had the choice of staying with the shoreline and going the long way around the bay, or going the direct route, straight up the middle. The first mile had been hard work, but staying on course had not been difficult and my fear of a capsize with Suzanne aboard had eased considerably. I would take the shorter way.

The wider lake gave the wind a broader surface to play on, and I could feel it testing me. I kept a steady pace, the paddle straight-armed down the right side of the canoe then rolled to the rudder position and away, twenty-eight J-strokes every sixty seconds like clockwork, a rhythm I'd fallen into over the years when straight-lining across a lake, the gear that worked best. The voyageurs worked at near twice that rate and for long stretches. Suzanne kept still and seemed to be enjoying the ride, oblivious to any trepidations I was feeling. She was getting a first-rate introduction to her first time in a canoe.

More cottages appeared on our right, many of them rustic like cottages should be, meant mainly for summer family fun. Some had flower boxes heavy with red and white and purple petunias that embroidered their windowsills. Weathered fieldstone chimneys rose against their clapboard walls, and it was easy to imagine a cheery fire in the hearth on chilly evenings when the sun had set below the tops of the pines and the lake lay black and still. There were flagpoles, some with flags aflutter, and all the cottages had docks of varying lengths and widths. Some of the docks were solid structures, others partially sunken or looking ready to break up with the next storm. People with drinks in their hands waved to us from their dockside deck chairs and Suzanne waved back, asking me who they were. Their friendliness lent an air of happy adventure to the beginning of our trip.

We passed the mouth of the bay and the cairn erected to the memory of renowned Canadian artist Tom Thomson, who painted here half a century ago. I had planned to show it to Suzanne and tell her about him, but it was away to our right on a point of land, not a good tack for today. I would leave it for the return trip.

As we drew close to the shore again, I eased up on the paddling. The wind appeared to be weakening. Above the treeline to the west, there were small but promising patches of blue sky. I never minded much if it rained the second day out or thereafter. It was all part of the experience. But getting soaked on day one before we had even reached our first campsite could make me grouchy. I was glad for Suzanne's sake that we seemed to have escaped a wet start.

Three aluminum canoes were headed toward us, two paddlers in each. In the first one, a small brown and white dog stood with its chin resting on a gunnel, watching us. I could see its stubby tail wagging to beat the band. Did they get the rain?

"Heavy this morning," the tanned, shirtless youth at the stern said.

"Been out long?" I said.

"Eight days."

The canoes glided past. The red and white stripes painted on the bow and stern identified them as rentals from the Portage Store. As the third canoe drew abreast, the bow paddler, a pretty young woman in blue shorts and a baggy-sleeved sweatshirt gave Suzanne a big smile and a wave with her paddle. Then they were behind us, the wind like a third paddler pushing them south, and when I glanced over my shoulder minutes later, they were already far down the lake.

We went around the bulging curve of the east shore. It was tempting to go straight ahead, up the left-hand passage that led due north to a series of portages on the canoe route via Potter Creek. It gave every appearance of being the way to go and could easily fool you. It was wide at its mouth and dotted with three or four cottages on either side. But I had made that mistake twice before and had to backtrack. It would not fool me a third time. I kept to the water on my right. It would lead us to our first portage and the dam at the north end.

Once around the bulge and protected by the trees, the wind died away and the air, stripped of its force, lay close, the water flat. I could feel my muscles relax. I lay the paddle across the gunnels and reached under the seat to retrieve the water bottle that I'd filled with orange juice before leaving home. Unscrewing the top, I handed it to Suzanne. From here to the portage, a short distance, we could take our time.

The juice tasted good but tepid, as would be all our "cold" drinks from now on. After a few days on the lakes under the heat of the summer sun, even the teetotaller can find thoughts of an ice-cold beer enticing.

A tiny grey spider scurried up the inside of the canoe. In a sudden movement, Suzanne jerked back and kicked her feet. I flicked it into the water, telling her the spider was a lot more afraid of her than she of it. We watched it float away, a tidbit for the first fish to swim by.

For the moment, we were alone. There were no other travellers in sight. I sat hunched forward, forearms on knees, and let the canoe drift in silence along its own course. After the strain of hard paddling for two miles, the quiet here was soothing. Brown-sugar sand mixed with rocks bordered the shoreline where jewelwing damselflies flitted in erratic flight, pausing to rest here and there on the tips of the grass growing in the shallows. The trees and thick undergrowth pressing the shore would harbour a plague of mosquitos, threatening any canoeist who dared to cross their shadowed perimeter.

I dipped the paddle again and ruddered to the right around a partially sunken log. Water droplets trailed from the tip of the blade, whispering on the water's surface. Suzanne leaned to one side to let her hand drag through its coolness. I shifted a bit to the left to bring the canoe back to level.

"Can we go swimming, Dad? When are we having lunch?"

In our passage between the green walls of trees, the humidity lay like a damp blanket, my T-shirt sticking to my back. A swim was definitely in order.

"We'll go swimming when we get to our campsite. We're almost at the dam. We'll have lunch there."

The towering white pine that marked the beginning of the short portage to the dam on Joe Lake came into view. It was a stately tree with sweeping long-needled boughs overhanging the water. I never passed it by without a silent greeting. To the casual traveller unfamiliar with Algonquin's history, it would probably seem ancient, but it was probably closer to a century old, because in the late 1800s all the trees hereabout had been levelled by the lumberman's axe, and white pines were prime timber. Photographs taken at the time show scenes of devastation that would resemble the First World War battlefields to come. The pine would have been little more than a sapling when the bloody conflict began in 1914, because it was only with the area's designation as a national park in 1893 (designation as an Ontario provincial park followed in 1913) that the miraculous recovery began. I could scarcely equate those stark black-and-white images of stumps and twisted slash with the rolling green paradise we were now entering.

The canoe slid across the pine's reflection, setting it in undulating motion. I let the bow drift in a slow arc to the left. There, nailed to a tree, was the portage sign showing the silhouette of a man in rubber boots with a canoe on his shoulders set against a yellow background, and the length of the portage, 250 yards, handwritten at the bottom with black marker. The landing it marked was broad and hard packed, room enough for a dozen canoes. The portage trail went up the embankment to the right.

The bow rose slightly as the canoe bumped ashore. I stepped into the knee-deep water and dragged it forward, then lifted Suzanne out and stood her down on the trail, still wet from the earlier rain. The portage, being a short one, would make for an easy carry.

Next to the landing was a dock. It seemed to have been there forever. In years gone by, you could pull up alongside to unload. It had been a boon to trippers, but their numbers and the vicissitudes of a northern climate had eventually done it in — roped off and posted with a Do Not Use sign. The dock was badly warped and partially submerged. The rot in its supports and planks could do serious damage to someone breaking through under the weight of a canoe on his shoulders.

I pulled on my runners and brought up the canoe pack, the two smaller packs and the loose stuff behind the seat, then lifted the empty canoe waist-high and walked it to the start of the portage. This particular portage was a key point of entry to the interior and thereby could be something of a bottleneck. Other routes branched off ahead, but here both inbound and outbound traffic converged. When canoes were numerous, a noisy convivial atmosphere could be generated among complete strangers, a confabulatory congregation of fellow paddlers of all ages, and reminiscent of what it might have been like in the heyday of the fur trade when the voyageur brigades happened to meet up. Over the decades, the heavy usage had widened the trail and made its surface akin to a roadbed. It ran a fairly straight line, parallel to the creek flowing from Joe into Canoe. Once upon a time the creek might have been passable, but the dam had restricted its flow, and what water did escape meandered among the rocks, making it impossible to canoe.

Interestingly, Algonquin Park maps from different eras mark the portage with different lengths. On my twenty-first-century map, the portage is shown as 295 metres (325 yards) long. On a 1974 edition of the map, the portage is marked as just 250 yards, so it looks like we didn't walk as far back then. In fact, the current map shows the portage after the dam, whereas the 1974 map shows the portage both before and after the dam.

After removing Suzanne's life jacket, I helped her get her arms through the straps of her pack, hung the binoculars around her neck and handed her a paddle.

"Just follow the trail," I said, pointing ahead. "I'll walk behind you with the canoe."

She dutifully turned and started out, a colourful sprite in green flowered pants, yellow pullover and red sailor's cap, marching off into the forest with her red vinyl backpack, paddle in hand. I donned my life jacket to provide a cushion against the canoe's weight, heaved its seventy-two pounds onto my shoulders, and followed. We would double back for the remainder of the gear and then break for lunch.

"Tell me if you see somebody coming our way." With your head stuck up inside the hull, vision is limited.

"Somebody's coming," she called back while the last word was still on my tongue. I edged to the right side of the trail. Three pairs of legs went past, one pair after the other.

The dam was a concrete structure of moderate size. The sluice gate, down about a third of the way from the top of the dam, allowed for a steady flow of water, but insufficient to permit canoe passage along the rock-strewn stream. The lake rose against its north side almost to the top, which made an easy deepwater landing for canoes pulling in to the shore, but you had to come in sideways. Straight on would leave the person at the stern stepping out into an unknown depth.

There were four canoes already pulled up and two more about to land. They were a mix of fibreglass and aluminum craft, the latter being fitted with thwarts fore and aft of the yoke in addition to the two seats. Their crews were busy unloading and carrying canoes and gear up to the flat ground where the portage began and where they had been stringing out everything in a line of packs, paddles, water bottles, footwear, life jackets, wet towels and disassembled fishing poles tied together with elastic bands.

Two boys, about ten years old, splashed along the water's edge, chasing a frog they were trying to snare with a fish net. As we rested and watched them, the sun broke through the cloud. I felt the burn on the back of my neck and hands. The weather in the park could change rapidly, and I was hopeful it had gotten the wet out of its system and we could look forward to a few sunny days.

"Ready to go back and get the rest of the stuff?" I said.

"He caught it!" Suzanne cried excitedly.

I looked to see one of the boys holding the net triumphantly in the air. They were both shouting and laughing at their catch, a huge bullfrog.

"Let's go see," I said.

It was brownish green and humpbacked. One leg hung down out of the net. The boy proudly lowered it to Suzanne's eye level so she could have a close look, but when I suggested she feel its webbed foot, she backed away.

We went back for the rest of our gear, walked it through and settled down in the tall grass to eat our lunch. Grasshoppers whirred about us. Orange bees made their rounds of the buttercups. A refreshing breeze came down the finger of lake we would travel next. For the moment, it was empty of canoeists, and under the sun and broadening sky, the water had gone from grey-black to a cool, inviting blue. I half expected Suzanne to ask again to go swimming. But she sat quietly eating her sandwich and looking at the water. She'd already had a full day. We had left our home in Montreal at four in the morning, driven for six hours to reach the park, spent an hour at the start point, then pushed through two hours of wind, waves and heat and made three hikes over the portage.

"See up there past the bridge where the lake goes around the bend?" I pointed in the direction we were going, curving my hand to the right. "We'll start looking for a campsite when we get around the bend. It's not far."

She nodded but seemed distracted, as though her thoughts were elsewhere. Probably dog-tired, which I was beginning to feel. She had taken off her cap. Her hair was shoulder-length and straight, and the summer sun had bleached it almost white. I dug the sunscreen lotion out of my pack, telling her to apply it when she'd finished eating and to keep it away from her eyes and mouth.

Canoe tripping has some built-in personal hazards, bears aside for now. On nice days, shorts and T-shirts are standard attire in a canoe, and out on the lakes in blazing sun you're like a strip of bacon in a frying pan. There is no protection on the water save for what you wear, so sunscreen is always a good idea. As for foul weather, unless I'm absolutely certain of a sunny day, I never pack the rain gear. It's either strapped to one of the packs or stuffed under the canoe seat where it is quickly reached in the event of a cloudburst. You don't want to be rummaging around for it under a cold shower. Hats are a good idea for both rain and sun. Suzanne's sailor cap was not the best choice. In the midst of our preparations, that detail, regrettably, had slipped my attention. You need a waterproof hat with a brim.

The popular baseball cap is not a good choice. And pay attention to footwear. In the canoe I'm either barefoot or wearing rubber sandals with capped toes. Embarking and disembarking at portages usually mean wet feet, and besides, if you capsize, hiking boots can drag you down. I never bring them on a canoe trip myself, but if you do, save them for the portages. As for the capped sandals, they prevent those nasty sticks and rocks along the trail from doing damage to your toes.

Hot, humid days and hard paddling will suck the water out of you, so dehydration is a risk. Back in the early 1960s when I first began canoeing the park, we kept a tin cup handy and just dipped it into the lake whenever we were thirsty. Our only concern was *giardiasis*, a common parasitic intestinal infection better known among canoe trippers as *beaver fever*. Symptoms can include abdominal pain and diarrhea. The ailment is not uncommon in many places around the world. I don't recall ever being affected by it. We continued to drink straight out of the lakes right up until the late 1990s without incident. Nowadays, compact pump-action water filters are widely used and take up little space.

On a cool, rainy day many years after my trip with Suzanne, I would get the shakes while solo paddling north on Lake Opeongo. They were uncontrollable, and as this had never happened to me before, it was scary. I knew I had to get ashore and get some heat into me. Fortunately, a nearby campsite was empty. I beached the canoe, got water boiling on my one-burner camp stove, pitched the tent and then tossed the sleeping bag inside. Without that camp stove, I don't know what I would have done. Considering my condition and not a dry stick of wood to be found, trying to start a wood fire would have been hopeless. Scalding hot chicken noodle soup never tasted so good. I downed it all, pulled on my hooded heavy sweater, got into the sleeping bag and soon was dead asleep. The crisis had passed. It has never happened since, and to this day I don't know why it happened then. I was warmly dressed and wearing rain gear. Sometimes the part of Mother Nature within ourselves is unpredictable, and both sunstroke and hypothermia can creep up on you. Kids can be especially susceptible and may not realize what is happening until after the symptoms have taken hold.

Since a medical emergency can happen at any time, a first aid kit is mandatory. In my younger days, when I was invincible and foolish enough to have travelled without a proper one, I was lucky and got away with it. Burns from the cookpot handle, splinters, cuts and insect bites are the standard hazards, but easily treated with a well-equipped first aid kit. I've found that a fishing tackle box makes a good carrying case for bandages and Band-Aids, scissors and tweezers, gauze, ointments, pain relievers and antiseptics, and whatever else you think might be useful. In decades of canoe tripping, there was only once when it was needed for a critical case where we had to paddle hell-bent for leather to our embarkation point and then on to the nearest hospital. The kit helped us stop the flow of blood from the lacerated leg of a fourteen-year-old. In the park you can be a long way from help. Best to follow the Boy Scout motto "Be prepared."

2

In the woods is perpetual youth.

– Ralph Waldo Emerson

The last two canoes landed at the dam. The two couples looked to be in their midfifties. The man with the greying beard walked off a little way and took a picture of his companions, framing them with the dam and the other canoes in the background. Their gear consisted of two canoe packs and two smaller backpacks. The two spare paddles were lashed between the thwarts and bow seats. The only loose items I could see were their cameras, water bottles, raincoats and route map. Efficient. They came up the embankment and sat down near us to have their lunch. One of the women said hello to Suzanne and asked me if we were just starting out.

I said we were, and the bearded man said they had been on the go for twelve days. They had started from Kiosk, an entry point on the perimeter of the park about forty miles northwest as the crow flies and considerably farther for the winding track of a canoe. He rewound the film in his camera.

"We had two days of rain," he said. "It came down pretty heavy this morning. Did you run into any?"

"No rain, but a good wind on Canoe Lake. If it's still blowing, you'll make good time."

"Are you enjoying your trip?" the woman asked Suzanne. The woman's face was deeply tanned. Crow's feet ran back from the corners of her eyes when she smiled. Strands of grey hair. When I nodded an OK, Suzanne quickly accepted her offer of a candy.

"Say thank you," I reminded her.

"Thank you."

"Just the two of you?" she said.

"Yes, it's her first trip. Did you come along the east arm?"

They had, she said, and I asked if they had seen any vacant campsites.

"I can't remember if there were any." She glanced at the others. "The rain might have discouraged people from moving on."

Even though all canoe trippers before heading out must inform park staff which lake they plan to be on each night, there are times when inclement weather, especially strong winds, make it difficult to keep to schedule. I went back to the canoe and had a look at the map. Up around the bend, eight or ten tiny red triangles indicated the designated campsites. Camping was restricted to these sites, which were cleared and maintained by park staff. For the most part, the sites were spacious and comfortable, but there was never a guarantee that you would find yourself a roost for the night at the site you preferred. First come, first served. I slid the canoe into the water and loaded up.

"Did you put sunscreen on?"

Suzanne shook her head. I applied some to her arms and neck and across her forehead and cheeks. It was closing toward midafternoon, the hottest part of the day.

"Where's your hat?" She felt her head and trotted back to pick it up from the grass. I held the canoe steady against the bank while she climbed in.

The bridge was a primitive structure of heavy logs and planks supported by rock-filled log cribs. The logs under the planks had been laid out with their bark on, but most of it had long since weathered away, turning the exposed wood to a slivery grey patina as the years dried and split the logs into hazardous-looking parallel cracks from one end to the other. The bridge was scarcely wider than a pickup truck, and it crossed the lake at its narrowest point. A railway line had passed through here once, the train stopping to let passengers disembark at the nearby Algonquin Hotel on a low hill overlooking Joe Lake. The railways heavily promoted Algonquin vacations. The cost of a week's stay back in the 1930s, meals included, was sixteen dollars, and according to one Grand Trunk Railway pamphlet, visitors would enjoy "the cool zephyrs of evening that waft from the lake [to] invoke slumber, invite pleasant dreams and make the dawn a blessing and an inspiration." This remains true, but over the next two decades, government policies in relation to this type of park accommodation evolved into returning Algonquin Park to its more natural state. The Algonquin Hotel and others like it within the park's boundaries have been demolished.

The bridge was low enough that even in a canoe you had to duck your head to float under. It didn't seem to get much use, but I always looked both ways, getting in three or four strong paddle strokes before sliding beneath it. The thought of being that close to the underside of a moving vehicle was not appealing. As we emerged on the other side, I scanned ahead through the binoculars.

Over long distances, it's often difficult to tell whether or not a campsite is occupied if the obvious signs, such as the canoe or tent, are hidden among the trees or behind the shoreline brush. You might spend half an hour heading across the windy expanse of a lake toward a site you had selected from the map, only to spot pots and dishes lined up beside the firepit or a clothesline strung with towels and bathing suits just as you're about to land. Binoculars are helpful in detecting these details before you expend the effort and time to get there.

There were two campsites about a quarter mile ahead. The binoculars found canoes pulled up at one of the sites and a dome tent tucked away among some pines at the other. As we advanced, a third site on the east side of Joe Island came into view, also occupied. I dug the paddle deep to get up momentum. The whorls of water created by the force of the blade made liquid sucking sounds as they trailed away behind us.

Suzanne sat cross-legged, her arms resting on the yoke in front of her. I asked her if she was feeling tired. No, she wasn't, and could we have a campfire when we got to our campsite. I assured her we would as we would need it to cook our supper, but she would have to help me collect the firewood.

"Do you have to chop a tree?"

I explained that we would collect dead wood from the ground. Cutting down trees was not allowed in the park.

The canoe slid easily through the water. I maintained a steady pace against the east shore. The excitement of our long day had not given us any time to think about being tired, but I suspected it would be an early night for both of us. Come sundown our sleeping bags would be looking pretty good.

We rounded the bend, which changed our course from north to northeast. The binoculars pinpointed four more campsites along Joe Lake's east arm. All showed signs of occupancy. At the farthest one, people were taking turns jumping into the water from the top of a boulder. We could see the splashes, but no sound of their fun reached our ears. With all of these sites taken and the real possibility that weather had stalled the departure of campers farther along, we could be faced with three more portages before finding a place to settle down for the night. We had been on the go for eleven hours and that was enough, especially for Suzanne, whether or not she realized it. I was concerned about her being out too long in what was now a baking sun. It was time to call it a day.

I backtracked slowly with the binoculars, taking in every foot of shoreline, and had almost come broadside on my right when I saw what looked like a bit of a clearing and a ring of stones indicating a firepit. I brought the bow around and paddled over. It was not a designated site but it looked well used. Sometimes a formerly assigned site may be closed down for a time if it looks to park management like it needs a rest, just like we needed one now.

I drew the canoe in sideways against a slightly submerged rock ledge and got out, instructing Suzanne to stay put and anchor herself by grabbing onto some shrubbery that overhung the water. A space slightly larger than our pup tent had been flattened out on the ground a few paces from the firepit and covered with a mat of ferns by the previous tenants in the hope it would give them a more comfortable night's sleep. The ferns were still green, and I doubted their wasteful (and illegal) uprooting had made a difference. The firepit was filled with wet ash and charred wood. It would have to be cleaned out and rebuilt along one side, where some rocks had fallen out, before we could use it. Not the nicest site, but it would have to do for day one. Tomorrow would take us farther from the reach of civilization and into the much bigger Burnt Island Lake with its numerous campsites. I steadied the canoe to let Suzanne step ashore, then got her to hold onto the gunnels while I grunted and wrestled the sixty-pound canoe pack to a dry landing. To this day, I have difficulty accepting the historical fact that during the fur trade days, the voyageurs routinely portaged two ninety-pound packs at once, and not infrequently, over long hauls. "*Je suis un homme*," they liked to brag. In his book *Fur Trade Canoe Routes of Canada / Then and Now*, Eric W. Morse wrote that aside from drowning, one of the commonest causes of fatality appears to have been strangulated hernia.

Our tent was a made-in-West-Germany pitched-roof model, which my parents had bought me when I was fifteen. It was more or less water repellent. It had no fly over the top and a really hard rain could pound through in an invisible mist that would have you turtling into your sleeping bag. It was wide enough to sleep two adults and had small porthole-style Perspex windows, about as big around as coffee mugs, sewn into the front and back. Two two-piece black metal poles, eight guy lines and a dozen pegs kept it upright, and if you were in the middle of it, you could sit up to change clothes. I had never been able to erect it without the wrinkles and creases at the corners, and I finally decided the problem was with the design, not the owner. Still, it bugged me.

I dumped everything out of the tent sack, poles and pegs clanking, and within minutes the tent was up and the sleeping bags tossed inside. Except for the food pack, the remainder of our stuff could be stored under the overturned canoe.

The site was spotted with blueberry bushes. Blueberries are a tripper's treat, and a couple of handfuls in the morning's porridge can help get a new day off to a good start. Unfortunately, the season had pretty much passed and the few remaining berries were tiny and tasteless and not worth the effort of bending over to pick. We tried a couple and spit them out.

Suzanne sat down in the shade of a cedar and rummaged in her pack for her Barbie doll and its clothes. I unrolled the groundsheet near the water and lay down to relax for a bit. It was good just to be still for a while. The sun burned into my arms and legs. I pulled my hat forward to shade my eyes. White specks of gulls circled far up against the blue, and from a high branch in the woods just behind, a red squirrel scolded us for invading its turf. The wind had died altogether and the scent of pine resin permeated the heat. Beads of sweat trickled down my sides like flies walking on bare skin. In a few minutes, we would pull on our bathing suits and go for a swim. I didn't feel overly tired, but for now it felt good just to do nothing.

It is a peculiar trait of paddling that it works the shoulder, arm and stomach muscles hour after hour, yet imposes little, if any, soreness or stiffness. I have seen this in myself with the first canoe trip of each summer and in others who have paddled with me on the first canoe trip of their lives, and I think it's because paddling is *doing*, and when engaged in its rhythm, we unwind. Thoughts of what happened yesterday or what we might have to worry about next week dissolve, and we drift with the canoe into the present. Water whispers along the hull. A breeze cools the body, sweating under the midday sun. Vision is reduced to the colours of blue and green. It is a clean and clear and quiet world with no distractions and no decisions to be made, and the mind, freed from the prison of its incessant chatter, rests. Physical strain passes unobserved, and unobserved, ceases to exist.

Paddling mimics childhood in that paddling is concerned only with the here and now, and in this mask, carries us imperceptibly back to a time when play was the heart of our existence and we chased every day in pursuit of fun. Paddling returns us to that chase and thereby to a freedom we had almost forgotten we knew. The wilderness is our playground, an enchanted world of exploration where the spirit of our childhood embraces us through its delight in everything we do.

I remember a little drama I saw on a solo trip before Suzanne was born. It involved two boys, about fifteen years old, and their counsellor, who would have been in his early twenties. Their stage was a three-thousand-yard outbound portage at the point where it began its ascent of a steep hill, a real challenge under a heavy load. As I approached with my canoe on my shoulders, I could hear the older one speaking quietly but earnestly, and the gist of his words implied that one of the boys had decided he wasn't going any farther. A good thirty minutes had passed by the time I deposited my canoe and walked by them again on the return trip to collect the rest of my gear. One of the boys, whom I took to be the unhappy camper, sat with his back against a tree while the other two sat cross-legged facing him. Two backpacks and a canoe pack lay on the ground between them. Normally, hellos would have been exchanged, but none of them looked in my direction and I kept my silence. As I went on my way, I heard the words "We're not carrying your pack. It's your responsibility." When I passed them for the third and final time, the boy against the tree hadn't moved. His companions were lying on their backs looking into the treetops. I don't know what powers of persuasion finally coerced him to carry on. Perhaps he just needed a rest or really believed there was no way he could climb that hill with his pack. But when his flotilla of canoes passed me the following day, he obviously had overcome the challenge of the day before and was paddling energetically along with the rest of them.

The teenage years can be a rough road. Had this reluctant camper been half his age, I wondered, would that rebellious scene have happened in the first place? Young children have a natural affinity for wilderness, and the earlier their introduction to it the better. They live lives full of imaginary adventures where lakes and trees and wild animals tumble around each other in a kaleidoscope of action. Real experiences in the natural world are an extension of the imaginary scenes they've played out courageously before. The line between fantasy and reality is blurred. "Courage," wrote twentieth-century journalist and philosopher Émile-Auguste Chartier, "is the king of fairy tales and the god of childhood." Children plunge happily into the wilderness environment, unaware of the metamorphosis that reality has sparked. And when they can experience it with their peers, it's even better.

One evening at the dinner table, conversation came around to parent-child relationships, and I asked my younger daughter, Laurie, who was then eighteen, what she thought was her parents' most significant contribution to her life. She considered for a moment and replied, "Giving me an appreciation of nature." Had she said emphasizing the importance of education or encouraging her toward her goals, I would not have been surprised and in time would have probably forgotten her reply. But her words caught me by surprise and I have always remembered them. Spending time in the outdoors and camping had been as natural a part of our family life as going to school or to work, and over the years I had not thought of this as exceptional. It was just something we did. But time has shown me that nature is indeed a gift we need to share with our children. It is a simple gift made extraordinary by the bond it forges between parent and child as they explore nature's treasures together. It is a gift infused with cherished memories and laughter that continue to warm the heart long after the embers of the last campfire have grown cold.

If "being lies in movement and action," as the sixteenth-century French essayist Michel de Montaigne said, then perhaps that is why paddling and portaging into the wilderness elevate our spirits and let us see things from an unexpected point of view, perhaps a child's point of view. Children are all movement and action, and when we, their parents, are thrown into the purely physical demands of a canoe trip, is there not at least the glimmer of a possibility that in this freedom of the wilderness, we could be seeing through a child's eyes? Cultural anthropologist Mary Catherine Bateson wrote that recalling childhood makes it possible to experience it again, and that some of childhood's experiences become the defining foundations of later learning. "The visions of childhood," she said, "can be treasured as alternative ways of seeing."

In the late 1940s when I was around seven or eight years old, my father was posted to the RCAF station in St. Hubert, Quebec. A few streets behind the house we moved into was a forest, and beyond that, farmers' fields. The fields and the forest became the playground for my friends and me, real cowboy and Indian country, where we carried cap-loaded six-shooters, slingshots and hazardous homemade bows and arrows my mother would not have allowed had she known. I usually played an Indian, for reasons I suspect were related to what at that age was probably a subconscious understanding of the indigenous peoples' close ties to nature. Feathers from my grandfather's chicken coop became eagle feathers, which I stuck one by one into a length of corrugated cardboard I'd made into a headband. I was a veritable Tecumseh, and together our happy troop roamed at will, raiding bird nests, digging out gopher holes, stalking invisible enemies, hiding out in the hayloft of a barn that we got to by sneaking on hands and knees through the farmer's hayfield, and in one instance, starting a fire in said field that scared the hell out of us. Luckily, we were able to extinguish it by carrying water from a nearby creek in our rubber boots. When a change of scene was needed, we rode our bikes a couple of miles down the road and climbed a gigantic willow tree, which we claimed as ours by hanging two bleached cow skulls from its branches. From here we could watch the freight trains roll past, charging dragons belching steam and black smoke not fifty feet away. I can't define what impact these childhood adventures may have had on my later life, but neither can I help but wonder if the seeds of my love for the outdoors, my subsequent lifelong interest in our country's indigenous societies and eventually the writing of this book were not planted in the explorations of those fields and forests of Quebec nearly seventy years ago.

 I swatted at a deer fly buzzing around my head, opened my eyes. The sun seemed to burn inside my skin. I stretched my arms over my head, then sat bolt upright. Had I been asleep? The lake. Trees on the other shore. I jumped to my feet. Suzanne's doll lay face down in the dirt with its clothes spread out beside it, but no Suzanne.

"Suzanne!" I shouted, spinning around.

She was crouched beside the firepit, poking at the ashes with a stick.

"What?" she said, looking up at me wide-eyed.

I took a deep breath. "I didn't know where you were. Was I asleep?"

"Yep. You were snoring. Can we go swimming now?"

The sun, I thought, was where I'd left it. Five, ten minutes ago? Surely it couldn't have been more. I felt the drumbeat in my chest subsiding. Travelling with a young child in a world of wilderness and water demands ceaseless vigilance. It can't be forgotten for a moment.

3

*Most of the things that are really useful
in later life come to the children through
play and through association with nature.*
– Luther Burbank

I floated on my back recovering from the shock of the water on my heated skin, moving my arms just enough to keep my face above the surface. Suspended, toes up, ears submerged, the world was reduced to the sound of my heartbeat and the colour blue. I was alone in the universe.

Wearing her life jacket, Suzanne sat in a shallow, bathtub-sized granite depression between the shore and the lake, making waves with her hands. I drifted over to her with a few lazy kicks.

"Time for a swimming lesson," I said.

"Can I take my life jacket off?"

I undid the ties and spread it out on the rock to dry.

She wore a red-and-white-striped bikini. In between the two halves I could count her ribs. She had weighed into the world at just three-and-a-half pounds due to complications during my wife's pregnancy. Her hospital wristband, which I still have, barely fits around my little finger. Whether or not this had anything to do with her subsequent fainting spells and seizures, we never knew for certain. My first sight of her was in a hospital incubator. She was wearing white hospital mittens and had an intravenous needle inserted into a vein in her head. A little pink bow was stuck to the tape that held the needle in place. It took three weeks of hospital care before she reached five pounds, the magic number for taking her home. She grew quickly, and for a while was taller than many other kids her age, a string bean with the accompanying awkwardness that could leave her tripping over her shadow.

"See if you can put your face in the water this time."

She didn't reply. Over the past couple of years, I had been giving her some swimming lessons by holding onto her waist and swishing her along the surface. She would dog-paddle, grimacing with head up and eyes closed, cheeks puffed out. I eased her into the water, supporting her with my hands at her chest and stomach. We went around in a circle.

"Don't move your arms and legs. Stretch your arms out in front like I showed you before and keep your legs straight."

She stretched out like a board. I went around slowly three times, lowering her a little bit with each rotation, and each time her chin came up a little higher. I raised her so that she barely touched the surface.

"OK, lie straight and put your ears between your arms."

I went around again, being careful not to let her face touch the water.

"That's the idea. If you were in the water by yourself like this, you'd hold your breath and you could float."

I sat her on the rock and demonstrated the deadman's float.

"OK, now you try."

She had her arms wrapped around her knees.

"Can I try after?" she said.

"Sure. You tell me when you want to try."

I dove back in, expelling air, then let myself sink feet first until I touched the muddy bottom. The water was cooler here, cold compared with the surface. In the heat of summer, trout spend their time in deeper waters, and you need to know how to fish for them. Casting a line from shore and reeling in won't get one sizzling in the frying pan, or at least it never has for me. I opened my eyes. The water, suffused with pine pollen, was a murky yellow. Looking down, I could see the fish-belly blur of my legs and feet.

Back in among the trees there was plenty of dead wood, including a birch log with scrolls of white bark curling back, a great fire starter that was often flammable even when wet. We could use this, I explained, as the tree had died, but she mustn't remove it from a tree that was growing. She peeled off three or four strips while I collected an armload of twigs and small branches and stacked them beside the firepit, then used my entrenching tool to shovel out the soggy ash.

"Can I shovel some out?"

"Sure."

I handed her the shovel and broke the longer branches into fire-sized length over my knee. The wood was damp, but it would dry quickly under the sun. I collected another load and spread it out to dry. Suzanne had wiped her hands on her bikini, smudging it with black ash.

"That looks pretty good. Are you finished?"

She nodded. A few more shovelfuls wouldn't have hurt, but I left it.

"You better wash your hands off in the lake."

I rearranged the rocks surrounding the pit until I had a couple of them in a position to support the metal cooking grill. These grills are sometimes found at campsites. We were lucky, finding one at ours. Although generally battered and blackened, they are an invaluable accessory in preparing a meal and preventing it from tipping into the fire.

By now lunch had pretty much worn off and I was ready to serve up the can of ravioli that I hauled out of the depths of the canoe pack, cranked open and dumped into the pot. At the touch of a match, the birchbark ignited. Dense white smoke poured out of the clump of pine needles Suzanne had piled on top of the bark, and in minutes a hot fire had the tomato sauce bubbling. The aroma sharpened our appetites. I handed Suzanne her pills and stirred the pot blindly, my eyes closed against the smoke. It was just on six o'clock, so we had three hours of daylight left. If we were up to it later, we could take a leisurely cruise along the shore. I gave the ravioli a few more minutes, then scooped it onto blue melamine plates and handed one to Suzanne. I tossed the can into the fire to prevent its aroma from attracting any forest inhabitants.

She ladled a piece onto her spoon, blew on it and downed it with her medication. I sat on a rock, balancing my plate on my lap. You don't realize how much you appreciate a chair with a back until you don't have one. Back muscles soon start to ache when denied this simple comfort. No matter how or where I sit — against a rock, a log, a tree or an overturned canoe hull — I can't stay long without shifting my weight to ease the strain running through the tail end of my spine. It would be easy enough to bring a chair. Small, lightweight aluminum camp chairs are available. I would never notice it strapped to the canoe pack. But for a long time I couldn't shake the feeling of wimping out. What kind of a tripper needs a chair? But the years take their toll. Eventually I changed my tune, and a camp chair is now a standard item on my list of camping gear.

As we ate our meal, I scanned the trees around us. We would need a long, sturdy branch twelve to fifteen feet above the ground to throw a rope over for hauling the food pack up. There were black bears in the park, and it was my personal experience that the odds of one paying us a visit during the night were excellent. They are first-rate scroungers and they know campsites mean food. A food pack left on the ground won't stand a chance, and once a bear is into it, trying to chase it off is a questionable option. The rule of thumb, which I have not always followed in the park and which shortly I was about to ignore again, is to avoid confrontation. When there is nothing left, a bear will amble off to the next site, and in the morning you can clean up the mess and head for home. Raccoons are a threat to your supplies too. Although they can climb trees and shinny down a rope to a pack, it's difficult for them to get any leverage with their paws while swinging in the air. On a previous trip, I'd been roused from sleep in the middle of the night by the distinctive sounds of their chittering communication. Unzipping the tent flap, I shone the flashlight up into the dark. Five bandit faces stared back at me, a mother and her four furry kits. They were clinging to the pack as it slowly revolved around and around at the end of its tether.

I mopped up the sauce on my plate with a bun and added a few sticks to the fire. Steam spouted from the kettle. Pouring some of the boiling water into the ravioli pot, I swished it around and left it to soak.

"Put your plate in the pot and keep your spoon."

Suzanne had cleaned up her supper, but like the chocolate ice cream earlier, the sauce was smeared around her mouth. I pulled a facecloth from my clothes pack.

"What's dessert?" she said.

"Applesauce and cookies. But I thought first we could go for a little canoe ride and have dessert when we get back. Is that OK?"

She nodded, but I could see she wasn't too happy with my answer, not because of the canoe ride but because of the applesauce. She knew I'd packed a few tins of butterscotch pudding, which was her favourite. We would save that for a special treat in another day or two. She would think about it and then savour it even more.

"Here, soak this in the lake and wash your face."

I handed her the facecloth. She went to the shore and dragged it through the water.

"Wait a minute," I said, suddenly remembering the movie camera.

Clicking off the lens cap, I zeroed in with the zoom. As the film wound past the shutter, I was unaware that the image I was capturing would be the one I would remember more than any other on the trip. A wisp of a child crouched at the waterline, staring unmoving into a movie camera, platinum hair and orange face, alone against a backdrop of sun-burnished lake and forest. It is one of those memories tucked away in the subconscious that in moments of reflection come back to us after our children have grown.

I hauled the canoe into the water. Empty, it rode an inch above the scum line that had formed in getting here. Suzanne lay her paddle across the gunnels like I'd shown her, and leaning on the centre of the shaft, climbed in and sat down. I pointed the bow toward the middle of the lake, and as I pushed off with my right foot, the keel bumped and scraped over a rock, leaving a blue strip of paint in its wake. I should have seen that rock, brightly decorated as it was with the colours of other canoes that had encountered it. There are painted rocks in lakes and rivers throughout the park, and sometimes if you're not completely certain that the shallow creek you're winding your way through is indeed the one you are tracing with your finger on the map, the multicoloured rocks just below the surface are helpful. You have only to look over the side for confirmation that others have been this way before you.

We slid smoothly along the shoreline. Out on the lake, the perception you have of your rate of travel in a canoe is that of a snail's pace. But when close to the shore, you're reminded by the trees filing past that a canoe is a speedy craft and two strong paddlers can cover a lot of miles in a day. To the Algonquins, who first inhabited the area, the canoe was indispensable, allowing them to travel freely through the endless forest country that was their home. Their birchbark craft, stitched together with spruce roots and caulked with pine gum, had for centuries plied these waters where aluminum and fibreglass now rule. Whenever I have a particularly hard encounter with a rock or partially sunken log, I think about those early travellers and wonder how adept they were at dodging them. I suspect their bark hulls took a beating, and the sticky business of repairing them was likely a commonplace.

I paddled slowly, ruddering around the end of an eastern white cedar that leaned horizontally from the shore. Cedar foliage is a nutritious deer food, and it is not uncommon to see a browse line along a cedar-studded shore, where deer have consumed the greenery as high as their outstretched necks can reach. You would think the park gardener had been at work with his hedge clippers, so perfectly straight is the trim.

The width of the canoe at the bow seat forced Suzanne to reach out to get her paddle into the water. I turned the camera to wide angle, and leaning back until I was resting on the stern, took in as much of the canoe as possible while keeping her centred at the far end. Without my paddle in the water to steer, we turned slowly in an arc. On the silent-movie film she looks over her red-life-jacketed shoulder in consternation and you can read her lips: "How do I make it go straight?"

We passed one of the campsites I'd seen through the binoculars. Two aluminum canoes were pulled up at the waterline and a third was turned upside down beside the firepit, where it served as a table, littered with food and utensils. The campers waved and called hello. They were roasting hot dogs on sticks over the flames. Hot dogs would not keep long in summer's heat, which meant that they were just starting out. I returned their greeting, then crossed over into a small bay on the north side. It was quiet here, except for the occasional camp sounds from the handful of sites in the area and the melodious singing of a hermit thrush hidden in the trees nearby. Its voice seemed to echo around us as we followed the shore around to the deepening shadows of the bay's west perimeter.

Suzanne sat looking into the woods, her paddle across her knees. At the start this morning, I had made her sit on the floor of the canoe, practically between my legs, and now there she was, alone on the front seat, just where she had wanted to be in the first place. She would have been quite safe after all, but this morning I had been anything but assured of this, and if I had disappointed her, it was only with her safety in mind. Better to err on the side of caution. Children are doers, and while you don't like to temper their enthusiasm, especially on a canoe trip, every now and then it's needed.

We drifted back into the bay and sunlight. Suzanne shaded her eyes against the glare off the water, then without warning stood up. The canoe rocked from side to side, almost throwing her out.

"Sit down!" My command was sharper than intended and immediately regretted. "What are you doing?"

She sat down, taking hold of the gunnels, head down.

"I want to turn around. The sun hurts my eyes."

"Never stand up in a canoe, OK? It's too tippy. Stay in the middle of your seat and bring your legs around to this side one at a time."

She turned around, not looking at me. It had given her, and me, a scare. It was my fault for failing to warn her of the hazard in the first place. I apologized for my sharp words and explained that canoes were a special kind of boat — they were not made for people to stand up in. We wouldn't want to tip over. A lesson learned.

By the time we got back to our site, the fire we had left as a bed of glowing coals was nearly out. I lifted the ravioli can from the ashes with a stick and hammered it flat with the hatchet. I would bury it in the morning. All that remained to do before turning in was to get the pack up a tree. After extracting some cookies and the applesauce and setting them on a log, I hoisted the pack onto my shoulder and told Suzanne to get the rope beside the tent. We marched thirty paces or so along the shore until we came to the tall pine I had noted during our after-dinner cruise. A thick branch about fifteen feet up was perfect — out of reach of Mr. Bruin. Black bears are good tree climbers, but unlike the raccoons, they wouldn't be going out on a limb and shinnying down quarter-inch-diameter rope.

 I uncoiled the rope, and using a slip knot, cinched a palm-sized rock to one end. Giving Suzanne the rope's free end to hold, I stepped back and heaved the rock underhand toward the branch. It fell short and hit the ground with a hollow thump. We needed to do this, I told her, so that mice and raccoons couldn't get at our food during the night. She hadn't asked about bears and I hadn't mentioned them. I threw again, and this time the rock went over the branch in a nice arc, trailing the rope after it to the ground. Using another slip knot, I tied the rope to the pack's shoulder straps, wrapped Suzanne's end of the rope around both my hands and pulled. A foot off the ground, I had to let it back down while I waited for the circulation to return to my fingers. A heavy pack is twice as heavy when you're trying to hoist it into the air by pulling on a rope over a branch, and this one was definitely heavier than anticipated.

 I brought the loose end of the rope around my waist, and with homage to my Boy Scout days, tied a bowline and tried again. This time it grudgingly submitted. Pressing backwards until I had it high enough, I tied it off around the trunk of a second tree. It spun around over our heads, safe for the night. It would get a little lighter each day as we consumed our food supply.

 The sky blazed in forest-fire colours along the dark western rim of trees, transforming the lake into a gently undulating orange blanket. Red sky at night — tomorrow should be a good day. With a reasonably early start, we could reach our next campsite by two o'clock. There would be three portages, but they were short and over level ground. It might even be possible to avoid one of the portages by walking the loaded canoe upstream, if the water level wasn't too low.

I put a few sticks on the fire, and after a bit of fanning with the cookpot lid, the remaining coals ignited them. We had our dessert, and after brushing her teeth, Suzanne went to bed without complaint, the rustle of getting into her sleeping bag hardly done before she was out like a light. I sat in the evening silence, poking at the fire and watching the silhouettes of bats zigzagging in their erratic flight after insects. For my part, they could never eat enough mosquitos. It is said the voyageurs paddled sixteen to eighteen hours a day because of the long distances they had to cover. It wouldn't surprise me if another thing that kept them going was the plague of mosquitos and blackflies waiting for them at every stop, especially in May and June when they were outbound to the west. Had it been possible, they might have preferred to sleep in their canoes rather than go ashore to suffer the whining, biting hordes.

Voyageurs are depicted in the Frances Anne Hopkins painting *Canoes in a Fog, Lake Superior, 1869* — the print that I'd seen on Andy's T-shirt at the Canoe Lake beach this morning. It shows three birchbark canoes disappearing single file into the grey mist of an early morning. In the canoe closest to the viewer, there are seven crew and two passengers who are believed to be the artist and her husband, Edward Hopkins, who was the personal secretary to Sir George Simpson, the governor-in-chief of the Hudson's Bay Company. The original can be seen at the Glenbow Museum in Calgary, and a large framed print has been a part of my home for decades.

Frances Anne Hopkins was born in England in 1839. Her voyageur paintings, which are based in part on her canoeing experiences with her husband in the thirty-six-foot-long *canots du maître* and the shorter express canoes, are considered to be an accurate depiction of that colourful bygone era. I wonder if she had to swat mosquitos and pick their limp carcasses out of her paints. She may have been reminded of her compatriot Anna Brownwell Jameson, who thirty years before wrote in her book *Winter Studies and Summer Rambles in Canada*, "Enough of Mosquitos. I will never again do more than allude to them; only they are enough to make Philosophy go hang herself and Patience swear like a Turk or a trooper." Amen.

I filled the pot with water and doused the fire. Flecks of white ash drifted into the air. In another hour the place would be floodlit by a full moon. Tomorrow we would be rested, and if we felt like it, and if the mosquitos permitted, we could wait up for the moonrise. I looked around. Everything seemed to be in order. The canoe was drawn up and turned over, and the clothes packs, along with odds and ends, were stored under it. There was enough kindling for breakfast. I'd brought a half-dozen eggs for the first morning and we had jam and peanut butter for the buns and there was powdered orange juice, hot chocolate and coffee. The pots, plates, cups and cutlery were clean and tucked away with the firewood under the groundsheet. The flashlight, bug spray and toilet paper were in the tent. Nothing left to do but go to bed, which in a few more minutes would be the only option as I could plainly hear the whine of mosquitos revving up.

I stood at the water's edge looking east. A spot of light flickered in the distance, pinpointing fellow campers through the enveloping darkness. I wondered how many other campfires burned in the park tonight, scattered like fallen stars over its three thousand square miles of lakes and forest, each one separate yet bound by the common thread of wilderness. What was it that drew people here and to wild places everywhere? What magic was it that made us want to spend hard-earned vacations sweating over portages and sleeping on the ground?

If a canoe trip teaches one thing to a child, it's perseverance. You can't stay in the woods forever. If you want to get back to the comfort of home and your own bed, you have to carry on. You have to deal with the bugs and inclement weather, the grinding portages, the seemingly endless paddling, the inherent bumps and scratches, the work of pitching and breaking camp, and all the chores in between, until at last you arrive back at the place where you started and discover not only that you had a great time but that you can't wait to do it all over again next summer. Such is the empowering gift of nature. "Something will have gone out of us as a people," wrote Pulitzer Prize author Wallace Stegner, "if we ever let the remaining wilderness be destroyed. We simply need that wild country available to us, even if we never do more than drive to its edge and look in, as part of the geography of hope."

American botanist, journalist and pioneer in agricultural science, Luther Burbank, a man credited with creating more than eight hundred varieties of plants during his lifetime, put it more bluntly: "If you violate Nature's laws, you are your own prosecuting attorney, judge, jury and hangman." Burbank was known and loved around the world for his work. When he died in 1926 at the age of seventy-seven, an estimated ten thousand people turned out to hear his eulogy in California. He gave his life to science and his discoveries to mankind.

Had he sought patents and monopolies for his achievements, it was thought that he might well have been the world's richest man. "The clear light of science," he said, "teaches us that we must be our own saviors, if we are to be found worth saving." Young minds imbued with knowledge of and respect for the natural world would have delighted him as no personal gain ever could.

Time to pack it in. I slapped myself top to bottom with my hat to chase off any mosquitos just waiting to start whining in my ear after I crawled into the tent. It had been a long day. A good night's sleep and a crackling breakfast campfire in the morning would be a great start to whatever new adventures lay in our path.

4

*Conversation enriches the understanding,
but solitude is the school of genius.*
– Edward Gibbon

A gull watched us from its perch on the protruding tip of a log a little way offshore, its pure grey and white form blending with the grey-white morning mist hanging over the flat, grey water. It knew campers to be good for a handout now and then, and having nothing better to do, it would wait and see.

Already I could feel the soft warmth on my shoulder, the sun working its way through the mist and cool air to warm the earth. Blue sky would be waiting just above the treetops. It would be a beautiful day.

After scrambled eggs and buns for breakfast, I set to breaking camp while Suzanne worked on the frying pan with soap and steel wool. I was careful to put all the smaller items in one place. It's easy to miss things you've tossed aside, like a tent peg or a coil of rope or the insect repellent, while you're busy packing. And once down the lake and over the portage, it would have to be something pretty important (like my reading glasses hanging from a tree branch, to give one hard-learned example from a later trip) to make me go back for it.

I loaded the canoe pack while Suzanne poured the leftover coffee and two more pots of water on the fire.

"Stir the ashes with a stick, then pour on one more pot."

It was important for her to understand that the fire had to be dead-out. While she busied herself with this task, I made a walkaround of the site to be sure we had everything and that we were leaving it as clean as a whistle. I carried the pack down to the water and balanced it upright against the canoe. Everything appeared to be accounted for. We were ready to go.

Suzanne had slept soundly. As usual on the trail, I had slept soundly for the first hour or two and again with the first hint of dawn. In between, I seemed to float just below a level of consciousness, which the tiniest scratchings could disturb, and I was often uncertain if these natural forest sounds had roused me from sleep or if I had already been awake when I heard them. I thought of it as *bear sleep*. The unfailing nocturnal visits of bears over many years of camping in the park had instilled an unease I couldn't shake. It was more a case of tense nerves than fear, for a bear's preference is to avoid contact with humans altogether, and a shout or the clanging of a spoon against a frying pan can send a bear skedaddling like a scared rabbit. But at the same time, you could never count on it.

A canoeing friend of mine, whose wife was not big on the outdoors, finally coaxed her into going on a long-weekend outing with him. They paddled to the far end of one of the park's bigger lakes, pitched camp on a small island close to the mainland, and after a lazy afternoon of swimming and reading and just lying in the sun, they sat down to the dinner he had prepared for the occasion. They were sipping their coffee and admiring a gorgeous sunset when Sara saw what she thought were two loons on the lake. How picturesque, maybe this wasn't so bad after all. As she watched, the loons made steady progress through the dappled water straight for them, and were a stone's throw away when the two heads suddenly morphed into the pointed ears of a black bear. Momentary panic as they dashed for the canoe and the bear waded ashore. Unable to resist the delicious smells drifting from the island into its neck of the woods, it had swum the short distance from the mainland to investigate. Everything was on the ground, and they could do little more than watch from a distance on the lake while it helped itself and then leisurely swam back to disappear into the forest.

"Well, are you ready to go?"

"Yep."

"Aren't you forgetting something?" I pointed to her life jacket lying at the shore. She pulled it on. I did the ties, then steadied the canoe while she climbed into the bow.

"Put your paddle against the rock and push out."

The bow swung out toward the lake. Using the momentum, I continued to force it around, past the rock we had run over the previous evening. I glanced back. The site looked just as it had on our arrival. I pushed off with my right foot, cranking out enough drive to lift the bow as I hopped in. The canoe slid away from the land with a soft swish of water along the curve of its hull, the wake dissolving quickly, erasing all sign of our passage. The gull, alert to our approach, lifted silently from its perch and headed east. I dug the paddle in and followed after it.

During breakfast, Suzanne had asked how far we would be going today, thinking perhaps of yesterday's long journey from Montreal to here. I had spread the map on the ground and pointed to the places we'd passed — the tiny black squares marking the cottages, Cook Island, the bridge where we had ducked our heads, the dam. And there was the parking lot and the highway home. It would be easier today, I said, because there was no wind and she could sit up front and help me paddle. We would canoe about the same distance as yesterday and camp tonight on Burnt Island Lake. She had questioned that, the name of the lake. I didn't know its origin, but maybe there had been a fire on one of the lake's islands a long time ago.

At a scale of two miles to the inch, the park map encompassed more than 2,400 lakes that first came to light as the grinding mile-thick icefield melted and retreated north about twelve thousand years ago. Only about 1,500 of these lakes have been named. The map was like a blue and green jigsaw puzzle stitched together with a network of pink lines for the canoe routes and red lines for the portages. If you stuck to the routes on the map, you would have to work at getting lost. The greater risk lay in hiking away from camp into the woods, where it would be easy to get turned inside out and lose your way.

Although I had been over this route a few times before, I kept the map handy. In a canoe you're like an ant in the landscape around you, but with a map you're an ant with a bird's-eye view. When you're on the bigger lakes, where the innumerable bays and coves can look much alike, your map provides the signposts that help you travel in straight lines and make fewer wrong turns. The other key is having a point of reference on the landscape ahead of you, an objective, such as a prominent tree or rock. When one objective is attained, you turn your sights to the next. You plot your course from this island to that point of land, past the campsite to your left, then around the dogleg where you have to keep to the south shore to reach the portage. One after the other, these reference points carry you along to wherever you've decided to go. There can be moments of doubt about direction, but with the map, and maybe a compass for overcast skies, you can always sort things out. At the end of the day, your reward is a good supper (all canoe-trip suppers are good suppers) and a feeling of achievement and well-being.

We coasted by the neighbouring campsite through a wisp of wood smoke, but did not see anyone up and about. The early bird who had started the breakfast fire must have been off searching for more wood. The three tents back among the trees and the three canoes at the shoreline meant that at least six people, maybe nine, occupied the site. If they were travelling today, they would have to hustle. The sun was already a thumb's length above the treeline.

We went past the entrance to the bay we had circled last evening and steered through a narrow opening between the north and south shores, coming out on the other side to Little Joe Lake. I drew Suzanne's attention to the lodge on our right side and the cars parked nearby. Numerous canoes and small sailboats with raised sails were pulled up on the beach. Again, there was nobody around, but bluish smoke was rising straight up from the lodge's black metal chimney and I pictured vacationers in overstuffed sofas drinking coffee in front of a crackling fire.

"Is that a camp?" Suzanne said.

"It's sort of a camp. It's called Arowhon Pines Lodge. People stay there for their holidays. You can drive to it."

"Can we stay there?"

"Not today. Maybe another time."

Arowhon was our cue to turn north and make for the stream that would lead us to our first portage of the day. It was also the last bit of civilization we would see until our return, and I was glad to have it at our backs. I had never been in the lodge but had heard that it was an excellent place to stay. Originally built in the late 1930s to accommodate parents who were visiting Camp Arowhon, a nearby summer camp for children, Arowhon Pines had been a survivor when so many of the park's other holiday resorts were being demolished twenty years later. Perhaps in another forty years or so, when my canoeing days would be done, I could relax on its veranda in a cushioned lounge chair, and as the younger generations paddle by, dream remembrance of things past. It was a sobering thought.

We entered the stream through a patch of water lilies floating at its mouth. Suzanne tried to snag one with her paddle. It submerged and came up on the other side of the blade. I stopped the canoe so she could lean over and pick one.

"There's a bug in it!" she exclaimed, making a face.

"What kind of bug?"

"I don't know. It's orange and black."

"It's a water lily beetle. They're harmless. Just grab the lily by its stem and pull it."

She leaned over, and grabbing the stem, hauled it into the canoe, holding it at arm's length. She would decide for herself if the bug was harmless.

I looked at the map. The stream went north for a short way, made a ninety-degree turn west, then north again on a wobbly track, and finally it bent around to the east where it went into minuscule Lost Joe Lake and then hooked up with Baby Joe Lake a hundred yards farther on. According to the map, we could paddle the first half of the stream and then portage the remaining 580 yards, skirting Lost Joe to arrive at Baby Joe. I would keep my fingers crossed that there would be enough water in the upper half of the stream to let me walk the canoe through with the gear and Suzanne in it. Three to four inches deep would be enough.

Here again, there is a variance between maps. My twenty-first-century map shows two portages along this stream, one of 165 metres (about 180 yards) at the ninety-degree turn, then a short piece of open water leading to another one of 435 metres (about 480 yards) that skirts Lost Joe before launching into Baby Joe Lake. On the 1974 edition of the map, there is no need to portage at the ninety-degree turn, so there is only the one portage that skirts Lost Joe, longer at 580 yards.

I folded the map down to the section I needed for the day and tucked it under a strap on the canoe pack.

"Let's rest for a while," I said.

I wasn't tired, but our repose among the water lilies on this soft, sunlit morning was the perfect opportunity for Suzanne to experience what for me was the essence of the park — its solitude and silence.

"Listen," I said.

After a few moments, Suzanne said she couldn't hear anything.

"Let's just be very quiet and then tell me what you hear."

She sat looking at the trees ahead, and the silence seemed to grow and fill everything around us — the lake, the forest, the sky — until there was only the imagined hum of light on water. We became part of the scenery, a brush stroke on a vast three-dimensional canvas over which we were free to roam as we pleased.

"What did you hear?" I asked when I could see she was getting fidgety.

"Nothing." Even though she shook her head, I was confident that nature was planting seeds in her young mind, and those seeds were quietly sinking deep roots. The gardens they grow last a lifetime. Edward Gibbon, the eighteenth-century English writer and historian, understood the value of solitude when he called it "the school of genius," a school that is hard to find in today's cacophonic world. The Algonquin Park interior serves solitude to you on a silver platter.

I've been blessed with countless servings from that platter. My journal entry from one morning on a mid-September solo trip describes one such serving: "Left campsite on Clydegale at 8:35 and arrived at Pen Lake end of portage at 9:20. No other travellers about. Paddled for about 15 minutes when a loon bobbed up from the depths about 15 feet in front of me and swam along looking back over its wing. The morning was perfectly clear, Pen Lake stretching before me like a mirror, the only ripple on its surface from the loon gone down again. The green, rolling hills all around and on the far shore a lone gull flying parallel to the tree line. And utter silence."

I remember that I stopped paddling to listen, awed that on so grand a stage I was afloat in absolutely total silence, watching the gull's languid, dreamlike passage along the distant green wall. Just the two of us in all creation, fellow travellers in the Garden of Eden. For early man, it would have been like this for tens of thousands of years. The modern-day assault on our eardrums is a sudden and dissonant storm in body and soul. We need to take a break from it now and then. The solitude of wilderness, like Shakespeare's sleep, is the soothing balm.

A dragonfly whirred past, its wings brushing my arm in a feathery touch, and alighted on one of the canoe-pack buckles.

"Look, Suzanne," I said quietly, pointing to the buckle.

"Can they sting you?" she asked, looking over her shoulder.

"No, they don't have stingers. They can't hurt you. They eat mosquitos."

This last point puts them at the top of the list as my favourite insect, in particular as they seem to have insatiable appetites. Their high-speed manoeuvrability and 360-degree field of vision make hapless, slow-flying mosquitos easy targets. "Winged bullets," one naturalist called them.

"Why does it have four wings?"

Good question. Why did it have four wings? Probably one reason for its quickness. I tried to think of another four-winged insect for comparison, but couldn't.

"I don't know. Maybe so they can fly faster to catch mosquitos."

We pushed into the stream. It was narrow and shallow, maybe two feet deep, and in places, choked with long grass that wound around the paddle blade. In streams like this, you tend to listen for oncoming canoe traffic around the next bend rather than watch for it. The murmur of voices or the muffled thump of a paddle against a gunnel give notice to press to one side. It is not uncommon in these passageways to suddenly come bow to bow with another canoe. Some fancy back-paddling and manoeuvring is sometimes needed to get around each other. But we were in no hurry. We had a good start on the day and we would be on Burnt Island Lake by noon. There would be time to find a campsite before the afternoon wind picked up.

"There's some sticks," Suzanne said, pointing.

I looked past her to see what she was talking about. Beavers had built a dam across the stream. It just broke the surface, a jumble of sticks that at this time of the year served little purpose as the water level on both sides was the same. Later in the summer when levels could drop, the dam would protect the beavers from predators by maintaining deeper water on the upstream side.

The slight depression at the centre of the dam marked the point where canoes were being hauled over. I got up as much power as I could with five or six good strokes, lay back to put more weight on the stern and let the hull ride up onto the dam. It got a good hold. I crawled forward over the canoe pack to Suzanne, being careful to keep my weight evenly distributed between the gunnels, and stepped out onto the dam.

"OK, put your runners on and get out on the other side. Better roll your pants up first."

She rolled them up to her knees and pulled on her runners, then gingerly stepped out. The dam was two feet wide across the top, so there was plenty of room.

"You can help me pull the canoe across."

I could have gotten the canoe across without her getting out of it, but this way she became a participant. Hand over hand on the gunnels, we pulled it over until it was mostly in the water on the other side. I got the camera out from under the seat and climbed onto the bank to shoot some film of her standing alone on the dam with the canoe and nothing else in sight but wilderness.

"Can we see the beavers, Dad?" It was a funny thing about Suzanne. You would think that she would call me Daddy, like other kids her age, but from the time she was around three years old, I was always Dad.

"Well, I don't know. They like to sleep in the daytime."

"Where do they sleep?"

"In their house. Remember how they cut trees and use them to make a house?"

She nodded.

"Maybe we'll see one."

So long as the water remained at a reasonable depth, the stream was an ideal home for a beaver family. There was bark from the nearby trees and green plants for food and an inexhaustible supply of mud for packing into their dam and lodge. Canoe traffic aside, it was a quiet place too, which meant that their acute sense of hearing would make it hard to get close without alerting them. I showed Suzanne the pointed ends of the sticks and saplings.

"They cut them with their teeth," she told me knowingly.

I steadied the canoe while she crept forward to her seat, then pushed off. Almost ten o'clock. Yesterday about this time I was parking the car at Canoe Lake, and six hours before that we had been sitting at the breakfast table back home. And now here. How easily and quickly we left it all behind, our virtual survival now pegged to sixteen feet of fibreglass and a food pack. Stegner's words came back to me, about driving to the edge and looking in. His reference was to wilderness, but he could have been speaking about how we often live our lives standing on the edge, never reaching our full potential, but ever hopeful of tomorrow. The experience of Algonquin Park and wild places everywhere can help children take that extra step toward their dreams.

Wilderness is the signature of Canada. In my lifetime, I have seen only a fraction of my country, but just knowing it's there to escape to inspires a sense of freedom. And it is freedom on a grand scale. To the northwest of our little stream, as the crow flies, lay the Beaufort Sea. In between, 2,500 miles of forest, lakes, muskeg, tundra, rivers, mountains and wildlife with not a whole lot of civilization along the way. In my mind's eye, I had paddled and hiked these places often — the Coppermine and Mackenzie Rivers, Great Bear Lake, Eagle Plains, the Barren Grounds. I could find them on a map like they were my own backyard, and in later years would have the good fortune to see some of that country and to canoe that fabled voyageur fur trade link, the French River, with my sixteen-year-old grandson Brian. Our capsize at the foot of Devil Chute with all our gear is a highlight we share. It is an immense and silent landscape, at times harsh and unforgiving, yet strangely enchanting. Stay there awhile and it gets into your blood. It challenges you and you can't forget it. Poet Robert Service called it "the spell of the north."

Rounding a bend, we disturbed a family of mergansers, a crested, rufous-headed female with her six ducklings. They were swimming away from us in a line, one behind the other, and keeping close to the bank. I whispered to Suzanne to put her paddle down. Without lifting mine from the water, I pushed the canoe ahead, hoping we could get a close-up look. Without even a backward glance, mother seemed able to gauge our rate of advance, and when I tried to close the gap she paddled faster, drawing her brood after her. We followed in their wake until they escaped down a narrow, grassy channel impassable to anything but ducks and the beavers who may very well have engineered it as a safe passage to the nearby trees.

A dead tree lay at an angle across the stream.

"Did the beavers cut it?"

I looked along the weathered trunk and could see where it had rotted away.

"No, it just got old. The wind probably blew it over."

There was just enough room along one side to squeeze past. I dug my fingers into the bank to pull us around and we carried on.

"There's the yellow sign!" Suzanne exclaimed, pointing to the start of the portage. The sign was nailed to a cedar that swept out over the stream in a graceful skyward arc.

"We'll see if we can get up the stream first," I said hopefully.

I got out and grabbed the bow. Despite the beaver dam farther back, the water barely reached my shins.

"Can I get out too?"

"Better not," I said. "It's pretty slippery."

Farther up, slimy moss-covered rocks and boulders in the stream bed would make footing treacherous. You needed to lean a lot of your weight on the bow and pick your steps carefully to avoid going down. She would never stay on her feet.

"I'll pull you," I said. "Maybe when we get near the other end it'll be better."

She had a way of raising the corner of her mouth and letting out a puff of air when she was unhappy with something. She seldom said anything, just the corner of her mouth and the puff of air, or sometimes a sigh.

The unmistakable screech of heavily weighted aluminum being dragged over stones came through the trees. Somebody upstream was trying to avoid the portage too. Were they coming or going? I waited, listening. Muffled voices, a shout, then another screech.

No need to wonder any longer about the depth of the water ahead. I walked the canoe in a half-circle and pulled it onto the landing under the portage sign.

"OK, you can get out. We'll have to carry our stuff through."

I carried the pack up to the start of the trail. It was muddy after the rain and studded with rocks and wandered off invitingly among the maple and birch trees.

"Let's take our packs through first," I said. It was easier to scout the trail this way before walking it under a canoe.

I helped Suzanne with hers and hoisted the canoe pack onto my back, not bothering with the tumpline as the distance was short. We each took a paddle. The morning had warmed up since we had pushed off from our campsite. Through the holes in the green canopy the sky shone a lighted blue.

We had walked a couple of hundred yards when the snapping of twigs made me look up. A man bent under the weight of a canoe pack was pushing his way through the bush on our right. When he saw us, he turned and hollered into the woods to an unseen companion.

"It's up here!"

There was an unintelligible shout back and the bang of aluminum on rock. The shallow water had grounded them, forcing them to unload in the middle of the stream and find their way through the tangle of bush and deadfalls to the portage. They would have to carry everything after all. I owed them a thank you for saving me from the same hassle. We got through the portage without difficulty, and when we returned for our canoe, two of them were standing in the stream watching a third member of their party approach with the now-empty canoe bumping and banging along the stream bed behind him.

In short order, we were back on the water at the south end of Baby Joe. From here we had a clear line of sight to its sandy beach at the other end, where people were busily moving about. Canoes were pulled up at the water's edge. I was hopeful they were homeward bound. I didn't want to catch up to any crowds moving our way, a crowd in these parts being three or four people.

"Hi! How ya doin'? Great day, eh! Been out long? How far ya headed?"

"Burnt Island," I replied as we landed.

"Well, you're there," he said, pointing to the trail behind him. "This portage is real easy. We've been out a week. Hell of a wind and rain the other night! The kids' tent blew down. What a mess. Ever put up a tent in the rain in the dark with three kids in it?" He laughed. "It ain't easy. Everything soaked and I mean s-o-a-k-e-d. The wife thinks she's got a cold. Spent all yesterday drying stuff. Lucky the weather was good. Then rain again last night with stuff on the clothesline. See any bears?"

Algonquin weather has a reputation for moodiness. In the space of two hours, I have seen it change from blue sky and stifling heat to black cloud and jackets pulled on under raincoats, with wind that pulled tent pegs loose as though they were little more than toothpicks. You went to bed with a prayer on your lips for morning sun.

I stepped out of the canoe. Our host was a man I guessed to be in his early forties. He was paunchy under his faded green sweatshirt and looked like he hadn't slept much. He grabbed the bow and hauled it up onto the sand before Suzanne had a chance to get out.

"Name's Merv," he said, holding out his hand.

"Bill," I said. "Heading south?"

"Guys!" he hollered at two teenage boys horsing around in the sand. "Get goin' and get the rest of the stuff. Hurry up!" He turned back to me. "Yeah, south. Our trip's done. A day early. It'll be late but plan on being home tonight. It's been a decent week despite the soaking. You won't believe it. We had bears three, four nights running, on Otterslide and Burnt Island."

He pulled a pack of cigarettes from a torn pocket of his Bermudas and a box of wooden waterproof matches.

"Just you and the kid?" He held out the cigarettes. I declined.

"Just the two of us. We left from Canoe Lake yesterday morning."

I glanced at Suzanne. She was wading ankle-deep along the shore and I couldn't tell if Merv's bear comment had registered with her.

"Good age to get 'em started. Get the campfire smoke into the blood early. My youngest, that's her over there, was four on her first trip. We do this every summer for a week, then hit the road with the camper trailer for the rest of the holidays. Been all over the province."

He took a deep drag.

"Where ya from?"

I told him.

"My wife's hometown — FLQ country!" he said, laughing. The smoke trickled out as he talked. "We're from Toronto. Good to get up here out of the traffic and smog, recharge the batteries. Fishing?"

No. I wasn't.

"I always bring the fishing gear. Never catch a damn thing but it keeps the kids busy. There's lures of ours snagged on rocks and sunken logs all over this park."

He took another drag, then pinched off the lighted end between his thumb and finger.

"Tryin' to quit. You don't smoke?"

I shook my head. He put the remainder back in the pack and folded the tinfoil around it.

"Lise says I should set an example. We don't want the kids picking up the habit. Trouble is I enjoy it." Lise was kneeling on a patch of grass near the trees, shaking sand out of wet towels and neatly folding them. Towels, clothes, sleeping bags and anything else that soaks up water add a ton of weight to your portage.

Two more canoes walked out of the portage and went across the sand to our left, the two portagers lifting them effortlessly off their shoulders and placing them in the water.

"You should have good weather," Merv said, looking up. "It's got the meanness out of it by now, I hope. How long ya out for?"

I said a few days.

His sons reappeared, loaded down with packs, paddles and life jackets, and dropped them and themselves to the sand.

"Come on guys, the stuff's not going to load itself. Did you remember the axe you left on the ground?" He hitched up his Bermudas. "Kids," he said, turning back to me. "Ya gotta keep on 'em all the time or they'll let you do everything. I guess you've been up here before?"

I nodded. "A few times."

"First time with your daughter?"

"First."

"We brought our dog up last year, or maybe it was the year before. Big mistake. He chased up a skunk. A trip to remember. Got a dog?"

I shook my head. I tried to see the time on his watch.

"Well, I guess we better get a-moving," I said. I reached down for my pack. Merv grabbed it and helped me lift it out of the canoe and held it while I got my arms through the shoulder straps.

"Nice talkin' to ya. Take 'er easy. Have a good trip."

5

Gie me ae spark o' Nature's fire,
That's a' the learning I desire.
– Robert Burns

The line of travel from the southwest tip of Burnt Island Lake to its opposite end on the northeast shore follows a gentle arc across four miles of open water. Numerous bays, inlets and points of land along the way vary the lake's width from a few minutes' paddle to as much as two miles. It is more than 1,200 feet deep. Personal experience ranks Burnt Island Lake right up there with bigger lakes in the park, like Opeongo, Cedar and Big Trout, as the home of the Old Lady. On a hot afternoon she likes to ride in from the west, testing muscle and mind of the canoe tripper. She can wipe out a week's worth of philosophical musings about man and nature in the stroke of a paddle.

The map showed the narrowest part of the lake to be at its southwest end, and as we paddled here, through the waterbound logs left over from the park's timber-cutting past, I pointed ahead on our right to the high mortar and fieldstone chimneys of Camp Minnesing. Almost hidden by the trees, the chimneys are all that remain of what was once a grand log building, constructed in 1913. A Canadian National Railway brochure from the early 1900s had billed the camp, or lodge, as "an ideal vacation place in the heart of an immense wilderness" where "the dining room service is of the highest order" and "the milk is secured from our own cows." I tried to sketch it out for Suzanne — its log walls, dormer windows and spacious veranda where people lounged in high-back rockers and Muskoka chairs, looking out at the lake. But it probably was as hard for her to see as it was for me to believe such a place had ever stood there.

In the 1920s and 1930s, Minnesing was used each summer as a Bible study retreat by Canadian missionary Dr. Henry Burton Sharman, who trained Christian leaders from around the world. From this wilderness setting, his graduates returned home to carry on the work of their Lord. I wondered about that, the connection Sharman saw between Christianity and this place. Had he felt here in Algonquin what William Wordsworth had felt in another time and place when he wrote about a presence that disturbed him with "the joy of elevated thoughts; a sense sublime."

The Minnesing chimneys marked the point where the lake opened up for the start of the lengthy paddle to its other end. On this morning, it was as flat as a pancake, the sun reflecting in a dazzling sheen from its glossy surface. I paddled slowly, just enough to keep us running smoothly through the mirror images of puffy cotton clouds, wishing someone was twenty feet above us with the camera on wide angle. It would look like we were canoeing in the sky.

The shoreline receded on both sides, and after a few minutes, I lay the paddle across my knees and let the canoe drift. There was no sound, not a whisper of a breeze or fleeting bird call from the wide scene around us. It was like a dream, where we floated on the air in a blue-green heaven suffused with brilliant light. Silence and solitude with plenty of elbow room. Ravaged by uncontrolled logging in the past, Algonquin had rebounded with renewed grace to welcome the adversary who once had overseen its devastation. If you take the time to look, remnants of the park's logging history can still be found on its lakeshores and along its rivers, including the wooden flumes built to bypass rapids and waterfalls as the timber was driven down the rivers during the spring runoff. It was in the late 1800s that a handful of people, including economists, foresters and early environmentalists, realized that the continued indiscriminate cutting of forests and subsequent farming of the Algonquin Highlands would cause serious problems to the region that was the source of a number of important rivers. Soil erosion was already evident as a result of these activities. In 1893, the park was established for the purpose of protecting the land and the rivers. Only selective logging was allowed, which ensured a sustainable forest and a refuge for wildlife. A century later, Canada designated Algonquin Park a National Historic Site, and today it hosts more than one million visitors per year from all over the world. One of the first green and white highway signs you see when driving out of Toronto's Pearson International Airport reads Algonquin Provincial Park 298 km.

I splashed some water on my face. The day was heating up, the heat cooking up a faint smell of canvas from the canoe pack. I panned the binoculars along both shores. There were plenty of campsites, a few occupied. This was a good sign. The map showed other sites scattered the length of the lake, so we should have no trouble finding a nice spot. I'd look for one about midway. We could use it as our base and do some exploring from there. It is always a treat on a canoe trip to have a free day to paddle around with no particular destination in mind, and then come back to a camp where everything is set up and there is nothing to do but go for a swim, eat, poke at the fire and watch the stars come out.

I aimed the bow at a small island near the centre of the lake and got us going at a good clip. On days like this, the big lakes are like broilers. Sunburn can be severe. One of the worst cases I ever suffered from had been on the tops of my bare feet. I hadn't bothered to apply sunscreen, and the hat, shirt and long pants I wore that day had not protected them from the sun's fire. The portages the next day had been painful. Defence against good weather can be as important as defence against bad. Black clouds and thunder give clear warning, but the potential misery hidden in brilliant sunshine is sneaky. Sunburn, sunstroke and dehydration may be your companions. Paddle smart, paddle safe.

I noted that two miles through the woods to the north of our position, the map identified what appeared to be no more than a duck pond as Baden-Powell Lake. It is ironic that the founder of the Boy Scout movement, British Lieutenant General Sir Robert Baden-Powell, should receive such minuscule recognition in this place, while a much bigger lake, and one of the park's prettiest, carries the name of nineteenth-century logging baron J. R. Booth. The park's timber made Booth a millionaire, while its healthy climate undoubtedly promoted his longevity. An old photograph shows him with white beard and cane personally inspecting a winter trainload of pine at the age of ninety-eight.

We passed the island on the south side and kept a northeasterly course into wide open water, riffled only by our trailing V and the brief sucking whirlpools created by the paddle. The whirlpools retreating and disappearing behind the canoe were markers for our rate of travel, the shoreline everywhere around us being too far off to indicate anything but very slow going.

"Look, Dad!"

Suzanne was pointing straight ahead.

"What do you see?"

"Some ducks or loons. Over there!"

It took me three or four seconds to find them. They were strung out in a long line, a wingbeat above the water and moving fast.

"How many can you see?"

She stared intently as though counting them.

"A bunch."

"Loons don't fly in bunches like that, so you know they're not loons. They must be ducks. Ducks flap their wings really fast."

We watched until they winked from view on the broad surface of the lake, simply vanishing into air.

The landing I had in mind was a campsite about a half hour straight ahead. It was on a point of land on the west side of the entrance to a small bay. If it was vacant, we would set up there, where we could see both sunset and sunrise and take advantage of those cool zephyrs the Grand Trunk had promised — lake breezes that could blow across to chase away the bugs. I rested my elbows on my knees to steady the binoculars and looked where I thought the site should be. There was no sign of tent or canoe, there or anywhere else along that entire stretch of shore.

Another island, Caroline Island, marked the apex of our travel arc, and once around it, we would see most of the other half of the lake. Pinpoints of bright light from sun glinting on wet paddle blades flashed in the binocular lenses. They were far away, as much as two miles by the map, the canoes low on the water. Unless they had made a lunch-hour start, the paddlers most likely had come through the Otterslide portage and were headed in our direction, but they would need to be closer to know for sure.

It was just on one o'clock when we bumped ashore at our site. I was glad for Suzanne's sake that we could get into some shade for a while, although she didn't seem bothered at all by the heat. I hauled the packs up, secured the canoe and surveyed the immediate surroundings. Roomy, and spongy with brown pine needles. I would pitch the tent facing the lake, so in the morning we could lie in our sleeping bags with the flaps open and look out. There was a good-sized firepit with a blackened grill on top, and beside it, courtesy of the previous campers, a small pile of twigs and split wood ready to burn. Two big logs carved with summers of camper initials and names had been laid down beside the pit for benches.

"Ready for lunch?"

I handed Suzanne the water bottle I'd filled by reaching as far down below the surface as I could, where it might be a degree cooler. She held it with both hands and took a long drink.

"What can we have?" she said.

We found a shady spot in the shadow of a maple beside the water. I spread some jam and peanut butter on a couple of buns and handed one to Suzanne. How the voyageurs managed the two-thousand-mile round trip between Montreal and Fort William in a single summer without jam and peanut butter is one of those bits of historical trivia that may never be known.

The shade relieved the sun's burn, but the sauna-like heat

remained. Sweat dripped from my forehead onto the groundsheet I'd spread for us to sit on. The breeze I'd hoped for was holding out. I looked at the lake. It was unusual to see it so quiet at this time of day, as though cowed by the sun's unmitigated intensity.

"When we finish lunch we should put the tent up and go for a swim," I said.

Suzanne nodded, her mouth full. Though she never put her face in the water, that never stopped her from wanting to play in it.

The tent could have gone up later, preferably toward evening when it would be cooler. It would take all of five minutes to have it ready. But trippers are creatures of habit, just like the animals whose forests they migrate through. They do things in certain ways, like how to arrange the gear in the canoe, establish the night's camp or tackle a portage. Once ashore I always put up the tent first, as wrinkle free as possible. Then the sleeping bags are laid in and unzipped about a third. Then the flashlight and the insect repellent are tucked into a corner just inside the flap so there will be no scrambling around to find them once the sun goes down. The clothes pack goes in last at the foot of the sleeping bags, where it is easily reached until ready for bed. This done, the site is officially mine for the night. There's still the food pack to hoist, but that's the last thing before turning in. It's a kind of territorial imperative, to be staked out with canvas and poles and a dozen steel pegs biting into the dark brown soil. Other canoes may pass by with a wave or the exchange of a few words, but they won't stop. I'm the king of my castle, a modern-day *coureur de bois*.

Water striders skittered at the shore, their minute bodies casting large shadows on the rocks a foot below the surface. Suzanne waded through after I explained they were completely harmless. We floated around in our life jackets and hats, squinting in the glare off the water.

"What should we do this afternoon?" I said, my chin just above the waterline.

"Swim!"

"After swimming, I mean."

"We can light the fire."

"We better leave that till suppertime. It's kind of hot now. Let's go up that way in the canoe and look around." I pointed to the bay.

"I want to stay in the water."

We stayed in the water without the slightest chill until our hands looked like prunes. I was glad to feel a bit of a breeze when we got out. It played on the lake, touching down here and there in shifting patches of darker blue. I gave her hair a good drying with a towel and retrieved our clothes from the tent. To the west, crenellated dark clouds crept above the horizon.

The bay formed a deep indentation that narrowed to a point and ended with a short portage. We coasted along its north perimeter through lily pads and under the branches of a gnarled, resin-oozing pine. The cooler air in the shade of the pine was thick with the smell of earth and damp moss. Suzanne said it smelled like spring. It was a heady, rich aroma that evaporated the moment we emerged again into the light.

There were three vacant sites on our right, and as we passed the third, a tiny cove opened on our left. Four orange canoes bunched up side by side rode there on the water. The occupants were boys in their early teens. A fifth canoe appeared out of the narrows just beyond. To arrive at this spot from the direction they'd come, you had a choice of three possible routes, two of them requiring numerous portages of varying lengths. I was curious to know which one they had taken

"From Big Trout," the stern-man in the nearest canoe replied. He was lean and tanned and semi-cheerful. He looked to be about eighteen. I surmised he was one of the counsellors. The crews were passing around a clear plastic bag of trail mix and a water bottle.

"Did you come from the Otterslides?" he said.

"No. Other end. Joe Lake."

The fifth canoe pulled in beside the rest. The guy in the stern was the oldest in the group.

"How does Burnt Island look for sites?" he said.

I said we'd been camped here since noon, so I couldn't be sure, but I hadn't seen much activity on the lake all day, and when we had come up the lake this morning, I'd seen a number of vacant sites. There were three right behind us.

"How long have you been out?" I said.

"Nine days. One to go."

Ten days on the trail. Herding a group of young teenagers over lakes and portages and seeing to their safety would be an around-the-clock job. As a counsellor, you would have no one to turn to but yourself in an emergency. Your training and inner strength would be tested. The two in charge of this lot appeared to have brought them through unscathed and were well away to getting them back to base camp suntanned and well fed.

"OK guys, let's go. Put the trail mix away."

"No high-grading!" one of the paddlers hollered.

"Never mind. Just put it away."

The high-graders are the trippers who root around in the trail mix for the tastier bits, like the dried fruit and chocolate chips. I've been one myself, I must confess.

The flotilla broke apart with a thumping of paddles on gunnels as the crews strained to get their loaded canoes up to speed. In the space of a minute, they disappeared around the point of land that formed the cove, and in the silence of their wake, it was possible to wonder if they had really been there at all.

I made a U-turn a few yards from the portage sign. As the bow came around, I saw dead ahead the domed shape of a beaver lodge. It was tucked away in a corner of the cove. Distracted by the canoeists on the way in, I hadn't seen it. I paddled slowly toward it, saying nothing to Suzanne, waiting for her reaction. With all the commotion, it was a certainty we wouldn't see any beavers, but she would have her first look at a beaver lodge. We were practically on top of it before she twisted in her seat to ask me what it was and then answered herself.

"Is that where the beavers live?"

"That's their house. It's called a beaver lodge."

I brought the canoe alongside. A freshly cut leafy branch lay across the roof, a sure sign the lodge had not been abandoned. I pointed this out to Suzanne.

"Are the beavers in there?"

"They might be. Or maybe they're swimming around somewhere waiting for us to leave."

"Where do they go inside?"

"The door's under the water. They swim under water and right into their house."

"I wish I could see them."

She looked over the side, her eyes scanning the water.

"We'll come back after supper. Beavers have very good ears, but if we're really quiet we might be lucky and see one."

We went once around the lodge. Here and there I noted a few rocks wedged in with the sticks and branches, and there was evidence of recent mud packing. A few feet below the surface, I could see the beavers' food larder from the previous winter, a tangle of peeled yellowish branches. It would have fed them through the long months when they were locked beneath the ice. I couldn't guess how long the lodge had been here, but with an abundant food supply at hand and a constant source of deep water, it would probably be inhabited for years to come. I figured we would have a decent chance of seeing a beaver toward evening, as they were frequently active then.

As we headed back around the point and got into open water, it looked for certain like we were in for a good old-fashioned summer thunderstorm. The clouds had really boiled up and seemed to be heading our way. They made a dramatic backdrop to the sunlit trees, an armada of towering sails blacking the ocean sky. The return trip to the beaver lodge might have to wait.

Gripping a gunnel at midpoint, I carried the canoe into the campsite and turned it upside down with the keel tilted to the west. Heavy weather frequently came from that direction, and in that position, it would provide some protection for anything I placed under it.

"Suzanne, see if you can find a rock about the size of the one we used last night for throwing the rope over the tree branch. Maybe there's one down by the water."

Twenty feet behind the tent was a huge pine with a thick pack-hanger-of-a-branch. I'd have the pack ready to hoist at the first spits of rain. Everything else could go under the canoe. If rain was on the way, the campsite would be shipshape and there would be nothing to do but lie in our sleeping bags and listen to it drumming on the canvas.

The clouds came with a flat-grey light that wiped away shadows and coaxed a few mosquitos from their ground cover. It was just past four thirty, too early for supper. On the other hand, if we waited, we might not get anything to eat at all, as there would be no cooking on an open fire through a cats-and-dogs downpour, and the earlier bun with peanut butter and jam would be short rations to last us until morning. I got the fire going and emptied a large can of Irish stew into the pot. The stew and more buns, which we had to use up before they went stale, some oatmeal cookies and a butterscotch pudding treat would be plenty.

As I hunched over the smoke and flames, stirring our meal, two gray jays landed on a branch a few feet away and tilted their heads from side to side as though trying to discern what was on the menu. They exhibit little fear of humans, and if you stand still with a morsel of food in an outstretched hand, there's a chance they'll zoom in and snatch it. In my copy of Roger Tory Peterson's book *A Field Guide to the Birds*, he describes them as "a large grey bird of the cool north woods; larger than a robin, with a black cap set on the back of its head, and a white forehead; suggests a huge overgrown chickadee."

There are more than 450 bird species in Canada, and more than half of these have been recorded in the park. In 2015, the *Canadian Geographic* magazine asked Canadians to vote for their choice for a national bird. Fifty thousand people responded. A panel of experts was then convened by the Royal Canadian Geographical Society to make its decision. The winner was the gray jay.

I found a stick and lifted the pot off the grate by its wire handle.

"Suzanne, bring the plates please, there, on the log."

She brought the plates and set them on the ground beside the firepit. I tilted the pot and spooned out the steaming stew.

"Careful, it's hot."

I tossed the empty stew can onto the fire and we sat on the ground with our plates on our laps and our backs propped against the log. It's amazing how good the simplest meal can taste when it's prepared over a smoky fire in the bush. Stuff you'd turn your nose up at back home acquires gourmet proportions as you pick ashes out of it and savour the hint of charred-wood flavouring.

The soft fluttering sounds of the gray jays in the spruce tree caught Suzanne's attention. "What's that bird?"

"It's a gray jay," I said. "But it has other names, like Canada jay and whiskey jack. The Cree Indian name for it is *wesukachak* — English people thought it sounded like whiskey jack."

"Why does it have so many names?"

"I don't know. They're called camp robbers too. They like to hang around camps and steal food."

The birds hopped among the branches of the spruce, seemingly intent on their own business but all the while keeping an eye on us.

"Throw them a piece of your bun and see what they do."

She threw a piece, and scarcely had it hit the ground when one of the birds dropped out of the tree and snatched it up in its beak. As it flew off, it bent its head down and transferred the morsel to its feet, carrying it away into the woods like an eagle with its prey, the second bird in hot pursuit.

The sky grew darker by the minute, but the air remained sultry and the mosquitos multiplied. How our pioneering forebears survived these devils while clearing land for homesteads is surely a study in intestinal fortitude. The tiny blackfly, also notorious in these parts, is no less vicious, but at least it goes about its business without that aggravating whine and has the courtesy to die off by the early part of summer. Mosquitos drag out their stay through the summer months, and a single one whining in your ear in your tent in the middle of the night can push you over the edge. I love the outdoors and readily accept its discomforts, but the mosquito is a challenge. To this day, the carcass of a British Columbia mosquito remains Scotch-taped to the first page of a journal we kept over a number of years on our family camping trips in the west. Reading my children's entries now ("I saw a cat fight a mouse," wrote my younger daughter, Laurie) brings up a lot of memories and laughter from those long-ago days.

I wiped my plate with the remainder of the bun and rinsed it clean with some boiling water from the kettle. Every can of food we ate made the pack that much lighter. Except for the strain of getting it stored safely up a tree, weight was not a big factor on this trip, since I was only carrying supplies for one-and-a-half people and all our portages would be short ones. Dried foods are the far better choice for larger groups and longer portages. In fact, if your route is a loop, try planning it so that the longer portages come near the end of the trip when most of your meals have been consumed. Dried foods are more expensive, but if you spread out your purchases between one summer and the next, the dollar impact is easier to handle and your back will appreciate it.

The boys in the five orange canoes we had seen earlier had come down from Big Trout Lake to Burnt Island Lake via the White Trout Lake and McIntosh Creek route. This route includes a series of seven portages totalling 4,860 yards, some of them beginning or ending in mucky ground. Those among the crews who doubled back on every one for second loads would have walked each portage three times for a total walking distance of 14,580 yards, more than eight miles. Seven times in short order, they would have unloaded, portaged and loaded up again through a hot, humid, buggy day — canoes, packs, paddles and all of the loose odds and ends that vex most portagers. It had been a challenge, but they had come through it only slightly the worse for wear, and in later years whenever any of them happened to get together, it would be remembered as a happy adventure, the pain forgotten. I peeled back the lid on the butterscotch pudding tin and handed it to Suzanne. She went to sit on a rock by the water, one leg crossed over the other, eating her pudding slowly, not wanting to scrape the bottom too soon. The stuff would have tasted better if it had been left to cool in a couple of feet of shaded water, but it was still a nice treat at the end of the day.

I scavenged around the perimeter of the campsite for an armload of twigs and threw a few on the fire, along with some pine needles. White smoke poured out as the needles heated up and ignited, choking off the mosquitos that my wood gathering had stirred into action.

"Can we have another pudding tomorrow?"

"We'll see. We've only got two left. Maybe we should save them for a day or two. When you're finished, remember to put the tin in the fire."

I cleaned the utensils and put a spoon in each of our cups, which were balanced on the log. If it cooled off later, we might have some hot chocolate before bedtime. She stuck her empty pudding tin on the end of a stick and shoved it into the fire under the grate.

"Are there bears here?"

"I guess there could be one around."

"Would it come in the tent?"

"No. Bears don't like to be around people. They just like people food."

She poked at the tin. Had Merv's words set her on this train of thought? Had she been thinking about it all day?

"If we keep the food up in a tree, they can't get it and they'll just go somewhere else."

"Will they go away?"

"They'll go to another campsite and try there. That's why it's important for everybody to put their food in a tree. There's lots of things for bears to eat in the woods, so they won't be hungry."

From the tone of her questions, I suspected she was asking mainly out of curiosity. The only bears she had ever seen were at a zoo, where they were either sitting up begging for popcorn, lounging in their pool or sleeping, hardly an animal that would appear threatening to a child. Her two teddy bears back home, one of them decked out in red plaid overalls, lent credence to the friendly image. She didn't say anything further and I let the subject drop.

Toward dusk I dampened the fire with a pot of water and slid the canoe back into the lake. The clouds that had threatened us since the middle of the afternoon had begun to shrink and dissolve, and I could see an expanding band of red sunset along the distant treeline. It appeared we were to be spared the rain that I thought was likely in the cards for us. With this good news, we headed for the beaver lodge. The breeze that had met us after our midday swim stayed with us, rustling the leaves and making wavelets at the shoreline, soft sounds that would help camouflage our approach. I cut directly to the south side to where the water was no more than a paddle blade deep. As we rounded the point, I whispered to Suzanne not to make a sound.

Sheltered by the land and the trees, the water in the cove was a glass-smooth black. The rippling V of a swimming beaver would be easy to spot. I lay the paddle gently across the gunnels and let the canoe drift toward the lodge. Suzanne sat stiff-backed and expectant, hands clasped between her knees. The sky directly overhead was royal blue, and here and there pinpoints of stars began to glimmer faintly.

In the half-light, I took it for a tree stump and had almost looked away. Then it moved. A beaver crouched behind a few tall blades of grass. So quietly had we drifted in, we'd caught it on shore where it was most vulnerable. I lifted the paddle carefully, and dipping it silently into the water, brought the bow around.

"There's the beaver," I whispered.

Suzanne acknowledged with a slight nod.

We were scarcely moving, but the gap was closing. This was a dilemma for the beaver. The animal was about ten feet away from the safety of the lake. We were three canoe lengths from the shore. It had to decide quickly whether to make for the water or turn and waddle into the woods. The latter choice was a desperate last resort. On land, the beaver was awkward and exposed to predators. Suddenly it made straight for us, hit the water with a splash and submerged. A trail of bubbles from the air trapped in its fur fizzed to the surface in a line heading away from the lodge. A loud clap resounded from the other side of the cove as another beaver slapped its tail in alarm. I twisted around to see, but the only sign of its presence was an expanding circle of ripples.

I switched the paddle to the left side, and with a few sweeping strokes brought the bow around and aimed it toward the lodge. As we drew near I could faintly hear the mewing of the kits inside.

"They sound like kittens," Suzanne said.

They did sound just like that, a plaintive little chorus from inside a mound of sticks and mud. There could be three or four of them. They would be about four months old by now. Here in Algonquin in the twentieth century, they were safe, but in the preceding couple of centuries, beaver fur was a prized commodity for the manufacture of hats, and the animal was hunted and trapped relentlessly. The early exploration of Canada is due in no small part to the pursuit of the beaver's coat. We were lucky to have had such a good opportunity to see one. We hung around for a while, hoping for another sighting, but they had either slipped inside the lodge or were biding their time off in the distance, waiting for us to depart.

Tight against the horizon, the sky had melted to an emerald green, my favourite time of evening. Straight up, more stars sprinkled the dark sky, flecks of light left behind by the sun. I kept close to the north shore and headed back toward the campsite, hearing only the soothing flow of water around the paddle and the scurrying of small animals among the leaves and twigs of the darkened forest floor. In the cooler evening air, the lake was a reservoir of the day's heat and felt warm enough for a bath.

Our campfire winked at us from its bed of ash and dwindling coals. It's a given that a campfire will be at its best for cooking after your meal is done. I threw on some pine needles and sticks and placed the kettle in the middle of the grate. The flames licked up with a cheery glow. I handed Suzanne a package of hot chocolate. She tore it open and tapped it into her mug.

"The water will be hot in a minute."

It was a few minutes after nine. In another hour or so the full moon would rise in silent brilliance out of the trees on the other side of the lake, magnificent and close enough to touch. If we could stay awake and were willing to brave the mosquitos, we were in a great spot to see it.

We sat with our backs to the log, staring into the fire, waiting for the kettle to boil. Somewhere on a highway heading south, Merv was probably smoking a cigarette and listening to the radio and trying to keep awake. I suspected he would be glad to get back to Toronto and his own bed after the bears and the rain and the blown-down tents. I wondered why he had been out here in the first place. He didn't strike me as the type of guy to take to the woods. Cigarettes, cold beer and a football game on TV back home seemed more his style. But who could say. You ran into all kinds of people out here. The two smartly dressed, middle-aged men with the little dog wearing a pink life jacket, probably up from the city. A German foursome who carried neatly sawn and bundled firewood over a thousand-yard portage. The two young Frenchmen who got off the plane in Montreal and made straight for the park. Within eighteen hours of leaving Paris, they had paddled their yellow kayaks nine miles to the north end of Lake Opeongo, and it being late in the day, had asked the group I was travelling with if they could set up camp beside us. And not to forget the young Japanese couple who had rented two canoes at the Portage Store, one to paddle in and the other towed behind on a rope with all their camping gear. We bumped into them in the middle of a narrow, grassy river way up in the park. I didn't envy them the portages, but you had to hand it to them. Intestinal fortitude.

The lid on the kettle started to rattle. I wrapped the dishcloth around the handle and poured a tablespoon of boiling water into Suzanne's cup.

"Stir that around and make a paste of the chocolate, then I'll put the rest of the water in."

Suzanne gave it a vigorous stirring and I filled her cup to half, then the rest with cold water so she wouldn't burn herself.

Merv had been right about starting kids young, to get that campfire smoke into their blood early. To this day, the smell of wood smoke triggers memories of family fun and closeness that are a treasure in our lives, memories that have helped us, even subconsciously, grow together through the years. A whiff of wood smoke on a rainy day or on winter's icy air reminds us of those happy times.

Had Merv camped as a kid, or had he started after he'd had his own family? Or maybe it was his wife who was the camper, and Merv, being game to try, had gone along. Certainly, that was how it happened in our family, only the other way around, and my wife's first family outing in a tent put her to the test. We went in June with another family to a provincial campground north of Montreal, pitched the tent in the rain, battled swarms of mosquitos and blackflies, shared with fellow campers the indignity of a less-than-clean one-holer-of-an-outhouse and watched a skunk wander through the site as we sat in front of a sputtering fire trying to get warm. That could have been the end of it then and there, and if we had called it quits, it would have been a poor gauge by which to judge the whole. We would never have recognized our loss. Only with the hindsight of future outdoor experiences all over the country did we truly come to understand how much the natural world had enriched our lives.

Never does nature say one thing and wisdom another, wrote Juvenal. If wisdom and nature are intertwined, then wisdom is bound to rub off on you in the woods, even if just a little. This is especially true for children. Like nature, they are direct and soak up the lessons she teaches.

When Suzanne was a year or two younger, we stood one day looking out her bedroom window at the swaying birch in the neighbour's yard across the street.

"Why is the tree shaking?" she asked.

"It's the wind. You just can't see it."

"Yes I can!" she said. "It's beside the tree!"

Who was I to dispute this? It had never occurred to me that the wind was there to see if you just looked. Where I had blinders on, she had seen clearly, and it is precisely this ability to *see* that makes a child's introduction to nature at an early age so valuable. The wisdom inherent in the natural world seeps into children the best way it can, without them ever giving it a thought. And along their road through life, it will stay around to lend them a helping hand.

I had thought of Suzanne's observation as unique until one summer afternoon twenty-five years later when I went for a walk with my four-year-old grandson. As we approached a hedge with thumbnail-sized leaves, he said to me, "It's cold out."

"It's cold? Why is it cold?"

"The bushes are shivering," he said, and sure enough the breeze coming along the sidewalk had turned the hedge into a trembling green wall.

I could hardly believe my ears, for I hadn't forgotten Suzanne's comment. Here was her observation coming back to me a quarter century later through the mouth of her nephew like some long-lost echo. This way of seeing the world is that of little children everywhere — straight to the heart of the object of their attention. Out of the mouths of babes. Their minds are clean slates and the influences they experience in their early years will stick with them. Our job as parents is to see to these influences being positive and motivating, and for my money, one of the best ways to tackle the job is to get them out camping and canoeing and imbued with the magic ambrosia of the woods.

I came to understand that little children, all of them, have the eye of the artist, and as my reading broadened, I began to find this way of *seeing* in the words of many writers. American author and spiritualist Dr. S.E. White wrote, "I have always maintained that if you looked closely enough you could see the wind — the dim hardly-made-out fine debris fleeing high in the air." He wrote numerous books on natural history and outdoor living, including some he claimed were received through channelling spirits. In *Anna Karenina*, Leo Tolstoy has the landowner Konstantin Levin comment, "Why, one can see and hear the grass growing." It is the road to adulthood that can chip away at this artistic gift, and for many children it will become a distant memory as they run the gauntlet of the "real" world. Nature can help them retain their creative spirit. "The invariable mark of wisdom," said Emerson, "is to see the miraculous in the common."

Whether he liked camping or not, Merv had been out there making the effort, and I wished I had been more neighbourly toward him. He had a big heart, but back in those days my inherently reticent nature had a tendency to short-circuit opportunities to get to know people better. Time and portages have whittled away at the failing, and I know if I bumped into Merv on the trail today, and wouldn't that be something after all these years, we'd have a longer chat. I'm sure I'd recognize him. I imagine he's the same. I would listen as he reminisced. We'd talk about the trips we'd made and the aches and pains that come with age. I'd enjoy that, and who knows. Algonquin Park is still my second home. If his cigarettes haven't done him in and the spirit of canoeing still catches him up, we might just meet again.

I poured the leftover hot water into the cookpot, soaked the facecloth in it and gave it to Suzanne to wash her face and hands. The fire had dwindled again to glowing coals, its faint light trapped within the circle of carbon-clad rocks. It was time to get ready for bed.

"Your pyjamas are in the tent," I said. "The flashlight's by the door."

I went down to the lake. It was pitted with the reflected light of stars. They spread like a field of daises to the south, over the route we had travelled in such brilliant sunshine this morning. The stars around and above Caroline Island and the distant ragged silhouettes of trees made the island look bigger than it had during the day, and I could imagine myself in the depths of an uncharted wilderness without any idea which way was out. "I have as it were, my own sun and moon and stars, and a little world all to myself," wrote Thoreau from his cabin on Walden Pond.

I called Suzanne to come and see the shooting stars. There were plenty tonight, rocketing through space every few minutes, igniting in fiery trails and vanishing in the blink of an eye. She wanted to know where they went, and when I told her they burned themselves up in the air, she wondered how air could make rocks burn. We watched them crisscross the heavens, pointing them out to each other with "there's one" and "there's another one," the mystery of their light glorified by the perfect silence in which it was beheld.

"The moon will be up soon," I said. "See over there? The sky is getting brighter. Do you want to wait and see it?"

"OK," she said, nodding.

I sprayed our hats with insect repellent. The smell would deter them for a bit.

We found a place to sit by the water, and it was not long before the brilliant orb rose out of the trees, looking ten times the size it would be when straight overhead.

"Why is it so big?" Suzanne said.

"Well, it just seems bigger now because it's low in the sky, and to your eyes, it seems to make the trees look smaller."

"The trees are big."

"The trees are very big, and when the moon is straight up over our heads, it will look smaller than the trees, but it will really still be the same size as now."

"Sometimes it's not round."

"That's because sometimes part of it is covered by the earth's shadow, like when the sun shines on you and you see your shadow covering the ground. You'll learn about this in school."

I told her about the first man on the moon, and said if it hadn't been so late at night when he landed, I would have gotten her out of bed to watch, even though she wasn't yet two years old. I told her the moon was a thousand times farther away from us than from here to home. She wouldn't want to go to the moon, she said.

The mosquitos were beginning to thicken. We went back to the tent and crawled in, zipping it shut quickly with the faint hope that we hadn't carried any in with us. The scattered brown spots on the canvas over our heads were reminders of past skirmishes with the murderous critters. We snuggled down into our sleeping bags, tired but happy with our day and thoughts of tomorrow's adventures.

I didn't know if I'd been awake already or if the approaching footfalls had roused me out of sleep, but unquestionably we had a visitor. As it drew near, I could hear the heavy breathing. Merv's bloody bear. I opened my eyes. Moonlight lit the west wall of the tent with a ghostly sheen. I turned my head slowly toward Suzanne. I could just make her out, lying on her stomach, head buried in her pillow, oblivious to everything but her dreams. The chance of a bear attack in the park is on par with being struck by lightning, but this salient bit of knowledge is cold comfort when you can feel the vibrations of the animal's heavy tread through the ground you're lying on. I could picture it sniffing its way toward us, neck outstretched, head weaving from side to side.

It went past the back of the tent, stopped, then walked away and stopped again. I rolled over and lifted the flap covering the back porthole to look out. The moon's brilliance had not penetrated the thick forest behind us. I couldn't see a thing. But I knew the canoe pack hanging from the branch had been discovered. I waited, watching the dark. There were a few moments of silence, then a wheezing and grunting like an old man bending over to tie his shoelace after a heavy meal. I was confident the pack was unassailable, that even if the animal climbed the tree trunk, it wouldn't venture out along the branch. And standing on its hindquarters trying to reach it from the ground, as it seemed to be doing now, was not going to work.

It came back, passing on the dark side of the tent, and went to the firepit. The cookpot rattled on the grate. I lay still, resisting the urge to look out the front porthole, not wanting to make any sound. It went down to the lake, splashed around, then came back up. The tent went black, the penetrating moonlight blocked by the bear as it stood contemplating its next move. The site smelled good, but how to get at the stuff. Rule Number 1: Never bring food into the tent.

I waited, laid out like a board, the animal's breathing almost in my ear. Suzanne slept on. Back to the firepit. A pot clattered to the ground. I had given the dishes a soapy washing and rinse, but to the keen nose of the bear, the smells lingered. I could plainly hear the lick-lick-licking. Past the tent again for another look at the pack, and then the unmistakable sound of it climbing the tree. I looked out the back porthole. Too dark. I strained to hear, picturing the bear all the way up to the branch, but then it was by the tent again. Bugger off, I told it under my breath. It must have gotten the message. Defeated, it wandered off, the thump of its paws diminishing to silence. I felt my muscles relax, like when the dentist removes the drill from your mouth and says all done. It was unlikely to return, at least not tonight. There were other campsites to visit along this shore where the pickings might be easier. I drifted in and out of sleep until the first hint of dawn, then dropped off into a slumber worthy of Rip Van Winkle.

6

So, there we were, on the way [from the Huron country] and in the dangers all at once. We were obliged to disembark forty times, and forty times to carry our boats and all our baggage amid the currents and waterfalls that one encounters on this journey of about three hundred leagues. At last, thirty-five days after our departure we arrived, much fatigued, at Three Rivers; thence we went down to Kébec.

– Father Isaac Jogues

Suzanne perched on the log, her bowl in her lap. I'd made the porridge thick, with plenty of brown sugar. It tasted more like dessert than a ho-hum oatmeal breakfast. It would keep us going till lunch, with enough left over for another meal. Even when you think you know what you're doing, it doesn't hurt to check the directions on the box. I filled my bowl and set the pot on the ground to cool.

The sun hadn't been up long. Angel slides pierced the foliage overhead, scattering pools of light on the forest floor. Dewdrops clung to the tips of pine needles, tiny diamonds catching the light and bending it into iridescent colours. Such power in those tiny drops, to colour the sun's rays. I stood eating my breakfast and looking down the lake. Around us the air was still, but out on the lake a light breeze was chasing up random patterns on the water. Perhaps it would stay with us to cool the effects of the midday heat.

I said nothing to Suzanne about the night's little drama. It would serve no purpose except possibly to alarm her. We'd finish breakfast, pack up and paddle across to the south shore where the binoculars had picked out an empty site. The plan had been to stay put, at least until tomorrow, but in view of the unwelcome company in the vicinity, we would make a tactical retreat and leave the site to the bear. Knowing that three hundred pounds of unpredictable teeth, claw and fur are loitering in a funk outside your tent flap in the dead of night because the food is out of reach is one of those camping vignettes you only laugh about in retrospect. I would feel more comfortable if we pitched the camp somewhere else. There was no reason to think it wouldn't be back tonight for another go at the canoe pack.

"What are we doing today?"

"What would you like to do?" I knew the answer.

"Go swimming."

"OK, but this afternoon when it's warmer. There's a nice campsite on the other side of the lake. We'll go over there first and put the tent up, then do some canoeing around and have a swim after lunch. Maybe we'll see another beaver lodge. How does that sound?"

"Why do we have to move over there?"

"Well, it's interesting to check out new places."

She scooped out a spoonful of porridge. "I need my pills."

I got the plastic vial out of the side pocket on my pack and tapped out two tiny pills. She put them in the porridge and down they went.

When we had stuffed ourselves, we washed up the dishes and within the hour were loaded and ready to go. We did a walkaround of the site. I kept an eye open for bear prints, but except for some vague sign of scratch marks around the firepit, the carpet of pine needles on the ground masked any trace of its presence. I wondered how many other sites it had hit during the night. There were eight or ten along this perimeter of shoreline, and it probably had its nightly rounds, scoring every now and then when some careless camper decided the food pack would be all right on the ground just this once. The Frenchmen in the kayaks who had set up beside us that time on Opeongo hadn't bothered to hang up their stuff. Maybe they didn't know any better, and the fact that we were on an island in the middle of a large lake had kept the odds in their favour. They left the next morning, food supplies intact. We never saw them again. Hopefully they didn't learn their lesson the hard way. On the other hand, if they had, it would have been a great story to tell back home.

We pushed off into the lake, as free as a hawk floating into space from a high tree. That first swish of water along the hull as the canoe sweeps forward into a new day is a special moment. You're fresh, your worldly possessions are at your feet, and with a turn of the paddle, you set your course for wherever you feel like going. Pierre-Esprit Radisson, the seventeenth-century Quebec *coureur de bois* and fur trader who, along with his canoeing partner Médard Chouart des Groseilliers, helped establish the Hudson's Bay Company, put it nicely when he said, "We were Caesars of the wilderness, there being nobody to contradict us." I aimed the bow for the east end of Caroline Island.

The breeze had risen to a stiff westerly, putting some chop on the water and buffeting the canoe, forcing me to paddle on the left side. It would be easier to head into the wind and go around the island's west end, then steer diagonally for the south shore. As I pulled hard to change to a southwest tack, my paddle blade caught the tip of a wave. Suzanne gasped and arched her back at the sudden cold shower, always a shock to the body and an occupational hazard for canoe bowmen everywhere. I encouraged her to dig in her paddle with all her might. Her efforts would make little difference but would make her feel a bigger part of the adventure. Together, she and the canoe pack did make for decent ballast to help keep the bow in the water.

Years later, on another trip north of Opeongo, a novice canoeist in our group went solo after supper to practise his paddle strokes. Two hours later and near dark, we were standing anxiously on shore and about to head out to look for him when he came into sight. He had gone downwind, and for over an hour had been trying to turn the canoe around to get back to camp. But the wind, moderate as it was, had refused to allow a lone inexperienced individual in sixteen feet of empty boat to do a one-eighty. So his laborious solution was to turn around in the seat to face the stern and alternately paddle on each side, left, right, left, right. Like closing the gate after the horse is gone, we suggested next time that he go to the nearest shore and load up the bow end with rocks. If you're heading into a wind, a front-end load helps.

But then, that's no guarantee either. According to Eric W. Morse, in his book *Fur Trade Canoe Routes of Canada / Then and Now*, the voyageurs were pinned down by wind on Lake Superior one day in three during July and August, and more often than that in the less favourable months. And they certainly had plenty of ballast and muscle. Their thirty-six-foot-long birchbark *canots du maître* weighed as much as six hundred pounds. Each carried a crew of ten plus another three tons of cargo, and according to the Canadian

Canoe Museum, they needed a pound and a half of pemmican per man every twenty-four hours to fuel their labour. Today, that would translate into something like eleven Big Macs or five boxes of Kraft Dinner per day. It should be no embarrassment for a modern-day canoe tripper to haul his canoe ashore to wait out *La Vieille*.

We rounded Caroline close enough to touch it with a paddle, and on the south side, came upon an unexpected sight. Crouched tightly to the ground as if to hide, and watching us with a crimson eye, was a loon. It lay very close to the water, and as we approached, I fully expected it to take the plunge and disappear. I wrestled the movie camera from the top of my pack.

The film shows Suzanne seated in the bow with the loon a paddle length away on her left. In the wind, it's hard to shoot film and control the canoe at the same time, and I confuse and upset Suzanne by barking orders to jam her paddle against the lake bottom on the right side and push so she can grab some bushes to anchor us. Unlike today's technology, there is no soundtrack to the movie film, so I'm the only viewer who really understands what is transpiring in those few seconds. Suzanne says nothing, but she is distressed about what to do, and in her confusion her left arm waves in the air, her fingers making a claw as if to grab the bushes she can't reach. I see it all again on the silent-movie screen, and despite all the intervening years, I remember painfully that thoughtless moment toward a little girl.

The loon was steadfast in refusing to move. I had never been so close to one and was puzzled by its willingness to stand fast at our approach. While it is master of lake and sky, it is awkward and defenceless on land. I could have reached out and grabbed it. As the film ran past the lens, one small head, then a second, appeared in the viewfinder from under the loon's wing. The reason for its stubbornness was revealed — it had chicks to protect.

It was a common loon, a nondescript name for a beautiful bird, and I much prefer its Latin scientific name *Gavia immer*. Its average weight is eight or nine pounds and its eyes are red only in summer, turning a dull grey for the other months. It is thought that the red colouring lets it see better under water and recognize other loons more readily. Unlike other birds, its bones are solid, which makes it a strong swimmer at depths of as much as two hundred feet. It sports a dappled white back, like sunlight on moving water. Loons are believed to mate for life and can live for twenty to thirty years. Every trip into Algonquin echoes with their repertoire of wailing cries. When I'm lying in my tent at night with a soft rain tapping on the roof, there is no sound more melancholy than the long, drawn-out, descending wail of a single loon from far far away.

There was concern about the survival of the loon at the time of my trip with Suzanne. A couple of years earlier, national television news had highlighted a scientific report that said pesticides were causing a decrease in eggshell thickness, which was leading to easier breakage. At the same time, peregrine falcons hadn't nested on the cliffs flanking the north end of the Otterslide Creek portage for over a decade, the birds having been wiped out of eastern North America because of the pesticides contained in their prey. And in case this wasn't enough, acid rain compounded the environmental threat, particularly in Algonquin, because the park contains little of the materials, such as limestone, that can buffer the effects of chemical poisoning. Nevertheless, after all these years the loons and the peregrine falcons have survived. As the current Algonquin Park canoe route map points out, the peregrines have made a comeback to their former habitat. Environmental controls introduced over the past few decades to curb the use of poisonous materials by industry and agriculture have had a positive impact.

I let the canoe drift off, not wanting to alarm the protective parent any further. What struggle with instinct had it suffered, not knowing whether to flee or defend its young? We carried on toward the campsite.

The new site was about the size of a large living room, big enough for our little tent, and lay between the lake and a ten-foot-high granite wall that sloped back toward the forest. The site jutted into the lake a bit, creating a good docking point on its west side. And right beside the water was a pine tree that looked like a good place to hang our food.

It was midmorning. There was no point in sitting around all day. We'd pack a lunch and do some exploring in the canoe along the shore. I had a look at the map. Around a point of land to the east was a marsh and beyond that a couple of tiny islands and the portage from Burnt Island into Little Otterslide Lake. We could head in that direction, hike the portage and back, then go for a swim. The Burnt Island end of the portage, I knew, had a sandy beach.

It would have been easy to carry our gear into Little Otterslide and then canoe into Otterslide Lake. But there were just the two of us, and I didn't want too many portages at our backs. Hindsight is twenty-twenty, and I would not council anyone to go it alone with a small child on a canoe trip for reasons glaringly obvious. If something had happened to incapacitate me, where would that have left Suzanne? It was probably what the woman back at the portage by the dam was thinking when, with raised eyebrows, she said "Just the two of you?" I can't remember if I had any misgivings at the time, but I doubt it. I was in my early thirties, physically fit and as comfortable in Algonquin Park as I was in my own backyard. But in the bush, there is no place for complacency.

The tent went up with its back to the granite wall, the door toward the lake and the pine tree. The pack rope went easily over the pine branch I had selected, but it would need to be closer to the trunk than I liked. The branch wasn't sturdy enough to support the pack's heavy weight if the rope went more than a couple of feet out, and there was not another suitable branch nearby. The pack would be within easy reach of any bear that went up the tree trunk. But daytime visits from bears were the exception, so I'd use the branch for now and go looking for a better one when we got back from our outing.

Once I had everything shipshape, I lay the groundsheet out and opened a can of tuna. We could have our swim and a sandwich lunch at the beach.

"Suzanne, empty your pack in the tent and we'll use it to carry our lunch in. Put your bathing suit on too. There's a nice beach where we're going."

This last bit of news put a smile on her face. She was ready to go in a minute.

We pushed off, the breeze at our backs. I kept to the shore, and as we neared the two small islands, we came to a pile of driftwood, a tangled mass of the bleached bones of long-dead trees. Years later, scientific researchers in the park would discover hemlock and white-pine logs submerged in Swan Lake that would prove to be over four hundred years old when they died in the early 1500s. They were apparently in surprisingly good condition because of the lake's small size, which inhibited damaging wave action, and its cold water, which acted as a preservative. Here were trees that had taken root around the time William the Conqueror stepped ashore in England to change the course of that island's history. The time of their demise would coincide with the arrival of Jacques Cartier and the planting of the *fleur-de-lys* on another island, known to the Iroquois as *Hochelaga* and to the French as *Montréal*. It would take three hundred years more for men like timber baron J.R. Booth to reach the land that would become Algonquin Provincial Park and just a few more years for loggers to decimate its ancient forests, virtually overnight. Square-timber logging reached its peak in Algonquin in the 1860s and carried on to the beginning of the twentieth century. Selective logging is still carried on today, but away from canoe routes and the sight of canoe trippers.

The water was scarcely more than knee-deep, and we got out of the canoe to poke around through the driftwood for a souvenir. It was fun to look for a piece that had been sculpted by water and weather into the semblance of a bird or an animal, some of the shapes needing more imagination than others. It made for great firewood too. I cracked off a few large bone-dry branches and lay them in the canoe.

"See anything?" I said.

She held up a piece that looked something like a fish with part of its tail missing, a quizzical look on her face, the exact same look her sister's son would have at her age. Grandchildren are fountains of youth for grandparents. They let them visit their younger selves. An expression, a gesture, a certain way of tilting the head or squinting at the sun can trigger forgotten memories. They remind us of the hopes and dreams we held for our own children, and in their strengths and needs we see our mirrored selves. The values that will carry them into old age are the same values we taught their parents and our parents taught us. The efforts we make today become part of future generations in the family tree. Our journey in our present lifetime is part of a longer journey that began long ago and will continue. Children are great imitators. We need to set high standards.

We waded around in our sneakers. Suntan oil washed off our legs and lay on the water in a rainbow sheen. I found nothing of interest, but Suzanne had collected a number of souvenirs, which she piled up in the bow. I asked her what they were. She didn't know. She just wanted them.

"Ready to go to the beach?" I said.

I helped her back onto her seat, moving her collection forward so she would have space for her feet, and we continued around the shore toward the broad swath of sand that marked the entrance to the Otterslides portage.

There was a single green canoe upside down on the beach. Green canoe, beige sand, blue water, backdrop of green forest. Clean and simple. A good photographer with the right camera and lens would capture it in an engaging composition. Often, the photographs I frame in my head are masterpieces until I hold the real thing in my hand. They are seldom looked at a second time.

Beach landings at a portage are a luxury, especially when you're sweating buckets at the end of a long carry. You can march the canoe and yourself straight into the water. But a greater number of the landings are rock and muck, and with a canoe rocking on your burning shoulders, you can be in trouble if you lose your footing. A slip and a fall can do serious damage to you and your canoe, which I can attest to first-hand (I had thought I had gangrene until I realized it was only algae stuck to the scabs of the wound on my arm). Caution is the password. Better for two people to handle the canoe together over those last few yards.

We rode onto the sand and I helped Suzanne with her pack. We would have lunch here on our return, but she wanted to carry it to the other end of the portage anyway. I slung the binoculars over my shoulder and picked up the water bottle and camera. We went up the sunlit slope of the beach and entered into the cooling shadows of the forest.

"He who thinks of coming here for any other [reason] than God has made a sad mistake," wrote the Jesuit priest Jean de Brébeuf in 1635 in *The Jesuit Relations*. He was referring to this kind of country, specifically the Ouendat, or Huron, settlements about eighty miles as the crow flies to the southwest of our position, where he lived and worked with his colleague Father Isaac Jogues for many years. They would have walked trails like this one, their long black robes sweeping the ground, but in the seventeenth century this was not vacation country. Just surviving the month-long canoe journey between *Kébec* and the Huron country was a major accomplishment. Once on the river roads, the Jesuits were dependent for their very lives on the goodwill of their Huron brethren. In a bid to enhance that relationship, Brébeuf took it upon himself to prepare a list of instructions for the priests to observe. He cautioned them about wearing their broad-brimmed Jesuit hats in the canoe, as they could obscure the view of the man behind. Once the Hurons were ready to embark, they must not be made to wait. The Fathers must not drag water and sand into the canoe with their robes, they must not ask too many questions and they should not undertake any activity, like paddling, unless they were prepared to continue it for the duration of the trip, which could be three hundred leagues, a distance of about nine hundred miles.

In another place in *The Jesuit Relations*, Brébeuf wrote of the Hurons, "forgetting the kindness I had lavished upon them and the help I had afforded them … and notwithstanding all their fair words and promises they had given me — after having landed me with some Church ornaments and some other little outfit, left me quite alone, and resumed their route toward their villages, some seven leagues distant." The Hurons, in fact, had landed Brébeuf at the former site of the village of Toanché, where he had worked in the past, and it was not long before he found the inhabitants who had moved to a different site, "which fortunately I came upon at about three-quarters of a league."

I look back four hundred years and try to imagine how I would have felt in the same situation. Abandoned in what was then truly wild country, with no map, no compass, no food, no means of transportation except on foot through almost impenetrable forest. It would seem a death sentence. Self-reliance and a powerful belief in God carried the Jesuits through incredible hardships, which would end for both Brébeuf and Jogues in excruciating death at the hands of the Hurons' deadly foe, the Haudenosaunee, or Iroquois, in 1649.

We took our time. Portage trails make for pleasant outings when you don't have anything to carry, and this one was only an eight-hundred-yard hike. You can enjoy the scenery and the feel of the earth under your feet, and if you're lucky, stop to listen to a white-throated sparrow. For me, its song is synonymous with wilderness, especially on a grey, drizzly day as you push your canoe along a narrow, grassy stream. The soft hiss of the rain on the river and those clear, sweet notes from the forest, the two together weaving a dream of a place unknown and far away. They are a bridge between present and past, the very sounds Brébeuf, Jogues and their Huron companions would have heard as they pressed on day after day after day.

Suzanne trudged along ahead of me, head down, ears and blonde hair sticking out from under her sailor's cap, red pack strapped to her back. I was following a forest pixie who would vanish if I made a sound or looked away for even a second. I raised the movie camera as I walked and centred her in the viewfinder. The clip is short, as I was trying to conserve film. I had only two rolls, and the second one was nearing the end. In those early days, when a hundred dollars was a big deal, five dollars per roll was expensive. In retrospect, what I do regret is not having brought along a still camera. That hundred feet of movie film I shot has lain dormant in a steel canister for a very long time, brought to light only recently as a research tool for this book. An album of photographs that don't need a projector, screen and darkened room would have been enjoyed far more often.

Beyond the Otterslide lakes lying at the end of this portage, the going gets a little tougher. There are two portage routes, one to the north and one to the northeast. The one to the north follows two-and-a-half-mile Otterslide Creek and is broken into five stages. At times you can find yourself up to your knees in black muck as you unload and reload your canoe, but it can be a good place to see moose. At the other end, you're rewarded with beautiful Big Trout Lake with its many campsites and islands. Just paddling its extensive, winding shoreline is a canoe trip in itself. The northeast route has three portages of considerable length that take you into Happy Isle Lake, where there is an excellent beach on the eastern shore.

After about twenty minutes, Little Otterslide Lake came into view through the trees. We went down the rock-strewn trail to the shore. A cedarstrip canoe, a rare sight in these parts, was just pulling in. A heavy-set man ruddered at the stern while his two crew, a young boy and girl, did the paddling.

Cedarstrips are beautiful craft, especially when new, but I never had any desire to own one. I was and always will be partial to the cedarstrip-and-canvas variety, perhaps because of their long history and because they were the ones I learned the craft of canoeing in during my camp counsellor days. I had even made one in my basement during my years in British Columbia. It was sleek, fast and highly unstable, and I was never able to stop all the leaks. Eventually I left it on the beach of a B.C. provincial park for anyone who wanted it.

I winced as the cedarstrip bumped off a rock and furrowed to a stop in the mud. The boy, about eight or nine, wore thick glasses. The girl, his sister I presumed, was a couple of years older. Both wore plastic whistles tied to strings around their necks. They stepped out one after the other and splashed ashore.

The interior of the cedarstrip was a sight to behold — loose stuff from one end to the other, a portaging nightmare. Unless they found some way to jam everything into their packs, they would have to make four or five return trips to get everything to the Burnt Island side. How far had they travelled like this? The man bent over to collect an armload, at the same time quietly reminding his crew to help. There not being a suitable flat spot at the landing, they carted the first load up from the shore and spread it out on either side of the trail.

Up close the canoe looked like it had seen the wars. There were dings and nicks and dents along the gunnels and hull, and here and there the wood had turned a dingy grey. Nevertheless, it appeared seaworthy. I couldn't see any water lying on the bottom.

"Are you going to the Otterslides?" the boy asked. I said we were camped on Burnt Island, that we were just out for a hike.

"That's where we're camping tonight. We just camped on an island for two nights."

"Did you catch any fish?" I said. Two fishing poles stuck out at the bow.

"We caught some bass. Just little ones. We threw them back."

The man nodded a greeting.

"How do you like the cedarstrip?"

"It's a good old boat. Needs an overhaul though. Some sanding and varnish wouldn't hurt."

He was right, but on the other hand, its wear and tear was the story of its life, gave it character.

"It belonged to my mother. She loved canoeing. It was her father's. She paddled me and my brothers around in it and now my kids are enjoying it."

He smiled and looked at the canoe. After a pause he said, "A lot of memories in that wood. If I had to make a choice between it and these two I'd have to think about it, right Brad?"

Brad stood beside his father with his arms folded across his chest.

"You'd pick me because I'm great!"

"Yeah, great for eating everything," his sister chimed in, her hands on her hips.

As we stood talking, a huge black insect buzzed our heads, making us duck to avoid it. It went around in a wide circle, too fast to discern what it was, and landed against a tree trunk ten feet away. Brad went to have a look, his sister and Suzanne following warily after him.

"It's a beetle or something," he said.

I was curious myself, but didn't want to appear rude by interrupting his father, who was expounding on the merits of his cedarstrip, something that was obviously near and dear to him. But from the corner of my eye, I could see Brad bent over, his face close to the tree, staring at the creature, whatever it was, and I thought how good it was for a boy his age to take such an interest. Suddenly, he stood back, raised his leg like a dog at a hydrant and delivered a karate kick. I heard the insect hit the ground, dead as a doornail.

"Gross," he said. He hunkered over the corpse, poking at it with a stick.

"You're staying on Burnt Island?" the man said.

"We've got a site about halfway down the lake on the south side." Seeing that Suzanne's attention was elsewhere, I told him about our bear last night on the north side.

"We haven't seen any but we met some people the other day who said they had one at their site."

Merv? I wondered. I asked if they had come from Big Trout, the lake after the Otterslides.

"No, just here. Tonight Burnt Island, then home."

Suzanne and I walked back over the portage with them, carrying their fishing poles and paddles, then waved goodbye from the beach as they disappeared back into the forest for a second load. Suzanne sat next to me in some grass and buttercups bordering the sand, and we ate our tuna sandwiches in the sunshine. Burnt Island Lake spread out before us like a three-dimensional Tom Thomson painting — blue sky and puffy clouds separated from the water by a narrow green band of forest and low hills. There was a bit of a wind, but nothing to give us trouble on our return trip. We would know around two o'clock if it was going to pick up. On days like today, wind conditions would often go one way or the other between two and two thirty. If you hadn't looked at your watch since breakfast, you could come pretty close to the correct time if you observed a sudden rising of wind on the lake.

I waded in waist-deep and demonstrated the deadman's float again, but Suzanne wasn't in the mood. She pretended to swim by walking with her hands on the bottom and kicking her feet out behind, taking care to keep her chin above the waterline. I warned her to keep watch for the sharp clam shells scattered about on the sandy floor.

It was an idyllic day, the world composed of water, woods and sky in a sea of air and light that brought every scene sharply into focus. I lay on my back with my elbows digging into the sand, the lake pulled up around my neck like a cool silk sheet. I looked to the southwest across the moving liquid plain, and at eye level, the water seemed to disappear before it reached the distant shore. To my right, an arm of the lake ran to the northwest for a mile, and on my left, the shoreline curved away for another mile into a broad bay. The two islands we had passed were visible, but sometimes an island in your line of sight can't be seen because it simply blends into the background of the mainland. You could be looking right at it and wondering why it wasn't where the map placed it, so perfectly did it meld with the forest behind. A sleight of hand that nature liked to play on trippers, and sometimes it could cause uncertainty about your route. Degrees of light can fool you too. Paddling out on an unfamiliar route in sunny weather and returning by that route under grey, shadowless skies can alter features in your mind and leave you guessing about whether or not you're really where you think you are.

I turned around to face the beach. The inverted green canoe looked like it had seen the wars too, another oldie. The gunnels were in rough shape, and toward the centre of the hull, a four-inch patch where it had been repaired. The butt ends of three paddles stuck out from underneath. As Suzanne and I and the cedarstrip crew were the only ones around, it had to belong to somebody at one of the campsites a few minutes' hike away on the west side of the portage.

"What are you going to do with those?" I asked. She was collecting small stones and lining them up at the water's edge.

"Nothing."

"Are you going to keep them?"

"I'm just seeing how many I can find." Holding one in her hand, she looked at me. "Can I keep them?"

"Pick out the ones you like best. You can put them in your pack."

The cedarstrip crew marched out of the woods with another load. I heard Brad ask if they could go for a swim when they were finished. They set everything beside the first load and disappeared again. By the time they got all their gear through, they'd be ready for a swim.

How many places are there like Algonquin where, without too much expense or preparation, a family can have the world pretty much to themselves with nothing to listen to but soft winds, birdsong and water lapping at their campsite shore? To those of us with a preference for peaceful settings, such sylvan landscape can become addictive, with each canoe trip ending in talk around that last campfire about next year's trip. Around the park perimeter, there are numerous access points where you can leave your car, register with park staff, load up your canoe or kayak and shove off on your adventure for a day or a week or more. If young children are part of your crew, you will likely favour sandy beaches. But they're not marked on the park map. You only learn where they are by making the journey.

For someone who has never been on a canoe trip, the details of such a venture may seem daunting, but in truth, if you're in reasonable shape it isn't difficult. First, go to YouTube and take a virtual trip. These days, trippers are recording their canoeing adventures and putting them online. Their videos will give you the lay of the land and a look at some of the portages. Then take a couple of canoe lessons to learn the basics. The J-stroke is the most important paddle stroke for lake travel. Its ruddering effect eliminates having to paddle on both sides of the canoe to keep it running in a straight line. Make the first trip out a two- or three-day experience with a short portage, perhaps, just to get an idea of what it's all about. Unless you're on the Petawawa River, which you shouldn't be, you'll be on flatwater. Take a tent and sleeping bags, basic foodstuffs that don't require glass bottles or metal cans, cooking and eating utensils, a gas camp stove as a campfire alternative, mosquito repellent, rope, water filter, bear spray, rain gear and a flashlight. And don't forget the toilet paper. Nowadays, in Algonquin at least, each site has a box-style latrine with one hole and a lid, located well away from the site. You get used to them in no time. Another way to tackle your first outing is a guided trip with outdoor experts. Again, just go online and you'll find them, as well as a list of what to pack for a canoe trip.

We dried off and headed back to camp. I crossed diagonally to the south shore and dawdled along, just out from shore enough to keep the paddle from striking the rocky bottom. The wind hadn't picked up with the afternoon as expected, easing our return, and near the shore, the lake lay calm in a sticky heat that had me wiping the sweat from my eyes. I could hear the water gurgling down the paddle whorls trailing in our wake, a sound like voices whispering. They could make you look around sometimes, so certain would you be that somewhere close by people were quietly conversing. They were my phantom companions on the lakes and I enjoyed their company.

7

I have always believed that the Canadian canoe is one of the greatest achievements of mankind.
– Bill Mason

We crossed the mouth of a small, triangular-shaped bay with a marsh at its southern tip and went around the point of land that curved out to form something of a protecting windbreak. I could see the location of our campsite not far ahead, so the marsh might be a good place to come back and nose around in this evening, just for something to do. Like an African watering hole, a marsh is often a good setting for wildlife observation. Maybe we'd see a moose before the trip was over. There were plenty of them in the park.

I moved a piece of our collected driftwood with the paddle blade so I could stretch my legs out from under the seat. We would have a good campfire tonight. The wood was dry and hard, and would burn hot.

"Dad! A bear!"

I looked at Suzanne, then to where she was pointing. We had come abreast of our campsite, and there it stood, a black bear sniffing and licking the ground right in front of our tent. I ruddered the canoe into a tight turn until we faced the shore maybe thirty feet away.

My first thought was for the pack, but there it was, still hanging from the tree. So what was the bear licking on the ground? I hadn't left any food lying around, just the empty tuna can. That had to be it! I should have washed the can out. The smell of that tuna drifting back into the woods must have drawn our visitor like a bee to honey. I aimed the camera, getting Suzanne in the foreground with the bear looking sideways at us, and pressed the button. It was a great shot until I heard the film clickity-click off the reel. Fini. I had gotten maybe five seconds before running out of film. Proof, at least, that I wasn't conjuring a fanciful story.

The bear, after glancing in our direction, went back to its sniffing and licking, unconcerned by our presence. We sat rocking gently on the water and watched. Its back was almost level with the top of the tent. It looked to me like a young bear. It didn't appear to have the bulk I would have expected to see in an older animal. I could see bits of paper on the ground around its paws. Perhaps I'd forgotten something after all, left something edible beside the firepit. Slowly I pushed the canoe to the right, past a pair of cedars growing at the waterline, and came around to the landing at the point where the campsite jutted into the lake. The bow bumped gently against a rock. I stepped out with Suzanne still seated and pulled the canoe in far enough to prevent it from floating away.

Now our visitor got interested. Apparently, we weren't just passing by. Its ears perked forward like an inquisitive dog. It stared at us.

Black bears, *Ursus americanus*, range throughout North America. They're solitary animals and omnivorous, which means they'll eat anything they can get their paws on. Camp food is especially attractive. At three hundred pounds, on average, they are the continent's smallest bear, but have a tendency to appear much larger and increase your heart rate when you're a few feet away from one with no barrier in between. Fortunately, in all my encounters with bears in the park over the years, they had always turned tail and run when confronted with yells and a clanging together of pots. I hasten to add, however, that this is not a given. I can't remember if back then there was such a thing as bear spray. Nowadays, I always carry it.

"You wait here," I said. "I'll chase him away."

I gripped my paddle in two hands and walked into the campsite. Without moving its feet, the bear leaned forward as if trying to get a better view of what was coming. The only thing between us was the firepit. Suddenly, it reared up on its hind legs and emitted a deep-throated "Whuff!" The white chevron of fur on its chest surprised me. I had forgotten about that. You don't see it when they're on all fours.

"Yah Yah Yaaah!" I hollered like a madman and banged the paddle against a tree trunk. Its forelegs hung down in front. I could see the claws along the edge of black fur, its beady eyes riveted on my approach. It seemed to tower above the tent.

When you're young and full of piss and vinegar, as they say, you're sometimes prone to do things that in later life strike you as extremely inadvisable. In the years ahead, this would be one of them. It was thoughtless and reckless behaviour. I had my five-year-old daughter right behind me. What if the bear had attacked? I should have stayed offshore and waited until it left.

I banged the paddle and yelled again. It dropped down to all fours. Was it coming for me? A long second passed as we stared each other down, then it turned and ran up the slope with me in brief, adrenalin-charged pursuit. It vanished into the underbrush. I could hear the receding thump of its paws and the snapping of twigs.

I looked around the campsite. Shredded bits of paper littered the ground, the remnants of a packet of powdered orange juice that the bear had been licking. But where had it come from? I looked up. The pack hung just where I'd left it. But as I walked around, I saw the slash in the canvas. The bear had climbed the tree, reached out and ripped the pack open. The orange juice packet had fallen out. It was this that had its attention when we arrived. More stuff looked about to rain down. As I feared, the pack was too close to the trunk. That, coupled with my mistaken belief that daylight bear raids wouldn't happen, had nearly cashed in our trip. Had we not shown up to spoil its day, we could have lost everything. How it managed to get its claws through that thick, tough canvas while the pack was swinging around was a demonstration of the animal's power.

I helped Suzanne out of the canoe, telling her to keep watch while I lowered the food pack and dumped everything out on the ground to reorganize our supplies around the damage. The attraction of the sugared juice crystals had saved the rest of the stuff, but how to get it all back in and keep it there, now that the pack had been ripped open? As I crouched over our supplies, frantically trying to figure out what to do, Suzanne called out in a matter-of-fact voice: "He's back."

I pivoted on the ball of my foot. The bear was sitting doglike on its haunches at the top of the slope twenty feet away, watching me, or more to the point, watching the smorgasbord I'd spread conveniently before it. I started throwing stuff into the pack as fast as I could. The tree was not the best, but it was infinitely superior to the present situation. The pack had to go up in a hurry. It couldn't be left on the ground.

"What's he doing, Suzanne?" I grabbed things randomly, not at all convinced they weren't going to fall out again as I hoisted the pack back up.

Suzanne, remembering her bedtime stories *Little Red Riding Hood* and *Goldilocks and the Three Bears*, replied with words I won't forget: "He's licking his chops."

"If he starts coming down the hill you tell me!"

I gathered everything up, stuffing it into the pack. Not only a bear at the campsite in the daytime, but one bold enough to return right after being chased away. This was unusual.

"Shoo, bear, shoo. Yah, yah."

I spun around. Suzanne was heading up the slope toward the bear, waving the paddle. I made a giant leap and grabbed her. The bear, intimidated by the commotion, took off again.

"Don't chase the bear," I said as calmly as I could. "When you see him you tell me, OK? I'll chase him away." My hands were shaking.

I worked the frying pan into the pack so that it blocked the rip in the canvas and put the pack in the canoe. No point, I decided, in returning it to the tree.

"Do bears like orange juice?"

"Bears like everything."

"They like honey," she said knowingly.

"What bear do you know that likes honey?" I said, wanting to mitigate the drama, more for myself than Suzanne, as she seemed unfazed by the whole thing.

"Winnie the Pooh."

"Lucky we don't have any honey. He might have got it."

"Will he come back again?"

"I don't think so, but if he does I'll just shoo him away. Don't you try to."

I was not that confident that it wouldn't be back. If it did return, we'd paddle off a little way and wait it out. We could break camp and try some other site, but what was the point. Obviously, there were bears in the area, and jumping from one site to another was nothing more than a guessing game. The key was to secure the food. Bears are ruled by their stomachs, and if they can't get at the food, they won't hang around. I positioned the canoe half out of the water with the life jackets and paddles in it at the ready, just in case. We'd have to wait and see if it dared to return a third time.

In 1881, on his wilderness farm halfway up the nine-mile length of Algonquin's Lake Opeongo, farmer John Dennison was killed by a wounded bear. Every tripper into the park knows this because the information is printed right on the park's canoe route map, which every one of us carries when heading into the interior. It is a sombre reminder of the potential hazard these animals can pose.

"Well, what do you want to do?" I spoke cheerfully, wanting to get Suzanne thinking on another track, which was easy to do. For her, the bear was just another episode in our camping trip, nothing to get excited about. She stuck out her lower lip and shrugged.

"How about playing with your Barbie for a while. You could get some sticks and make a tent for her."

This sounded like a good idea to her. She rounded up her doll and its wardrobe. I pulled my dog-eared copy of *The Seven Pillars of Wisdom* from the clothes pack, a book I had wanted to read ever since seeing David Lean's film *Lawrence of Arabia*, and sat on the ground with my back against a granite boulder near the water, but my attention wandered, replaying the bear scene and Suzanne's run at it with the paddle. To put an old head on young shoulders. As novice parents, we sometimes do not truly understand the impact our words and actions can have on our children. What we say and do in their presence makes its imprint. Whatever road we choose to take, they will be our passengers in one way or another.

Like many, I suspect, I like to think I'm wiser as a grandparent. I see the error of my ways (some of them) and if I could do it all over again, there are things I would do differently in the raising of my children. I'm willing to bet most parents feel the same. How many of us are truly prepared for the job in the first place?

I have a sense of being more attuned to the growth of my grandchildren than I was to that of my own children. Maybe it's just experience with living. As a parent, I suspect I was too busy doing the talking and not taking the time to listen and observe. Age grants us a degree of insight, and with a steadier hand on the helm, we can help steer our grandchildren along the right road. We can do this simply by being there for them, by showing that we are interested in the everyday things shaping their lives and by letting them know, in our own way, how much we love them. And, of course, when they get unruly, simply give them back to Mum and Dad.

I watched Suzanne as she walked around bent over, picking up sticks for her Barbie tent. Her matter-of-fact offensive against the bear got me to thinking. For her, the trip was not a conscious one. By that, I mean she was not consciously impressed by the wilderness around her. It was just there and things just happened and she was having fun, just as she would at the playground near our house. Her head was unencumbered by adjectives. Where I saw storm warnings as the billowing sails of galleons in the sea-blue sky, she saw clouds. The towering dark green masts of pines were trees. The warm silky feel of the lake was water to swim in. I wondered which of us saw things more clearly. Little children have a bit of the philosopher in them. How often have we acknowledged this with the expression "out of the mouths of babes"? In their minds, the truth is everywhere they look, and before we've taught them otherwise, they express themselves freely. We need to take the time to listen. We might learn a thing or two.

"Dad, can you help me?"

She had a fistful of sticks for her Barbie tent. I closed the book where I'd opened it.

"Where do you want to put it?" I said.

"Here."

She was standing in the middle of the campsite. It was on the tip of my tongue to say it would be better off to the side so we wouldn't trip over it.

"OK, get some pine needles for the floor."

I selected the three longest sticks, broke them off about a foot long and made a tripod.

"You can balance the other sticks against these three all the way around, then you'll have a teepee. Leave a space for the floor."

She spread out the needles. I showed her how to measure the sticks for the right length.

"OK, now you do the rest. I'll get some stones. We can make a firepit too."

"Can we have a fire in it?"

"Hmm, we'll see."

The project grew. Once one thing was done, we'd think of something else. Birchbark was added to the teepee, and I made a flag from a piece of the orange juice paper. A stick palisade went up around the teepee to defend it against enemy attack, and then a spoon-dredged moat with a bridge circled the palisade. Suzanne filled it with water. A path went down from the bridge to the lake. We lined it on both sides with weeds and her stones from the beach, all of which she had decided to keep.

When we figured we had done everything we could, I went back to my book while Suzanne put Barbie through her adventures. Had there been a way to do it, I'd have made a Ken out of twigs, but that was beyond my skill set. Barbie would have to go it alone.

All the time we'd been busy, I'd kept an eye open for the bear, and while it hadn't returned, I held out little hope that we had seen the last of it. The canoe pack, having been breached for those tasty orange crystals, would be a lure hard to resist. The only effective deterrent would be to make it impossible for the bear to reach.

It was nearly five o'clock. I should probably rustle up some grub. The late afternoon heat had imbued a feeling of indolence. All I really wanted was a drink with ice. It was hard to imagine on a day like this that six months from now the temperature at this very spot could be thirty degrees below zero. On that account alone, you had to admire the indigenous people who survived here in earlier times, the thin bark of their houses and a smoky fire their only protection against the bitter cold.

The year Brébeuf left for the Huron country, another of his colleagues, Father Paul Le Jeune, wintered with the Montagnais on the north shore of the St. Lawrence River. Le Jeune recorded the following in *The Jesuit Relations*: "You cannot stand upright in this house [wigwam] as much on account of its low roof as the suffocating smoke; and consequently you must always lie down, or sit flat upon the ground, the usual posture of the Savages. When you go out, the cold, the snow, and the danger of getting lost in these great woods drive you in again more quickly than the wind and keep you a prisoner in a dungeon which has neither lock nor key."

But as bad as the cold was, it paled in comparison with the choking smoke from the fire they needed to keep from freezing to death: "As to the smoke I confess to you that it is a martyrdom. It almost killed me, and made me weep continually, though I had neither grief nor sadness in my heart. It sometimes grounded all of us who were in the [house]; that is, it caused us to place our mouths against the earth in order to breathe; as it were to eat the earth, so as not to eat the smoke. I have sometimes remained several hours in that position, especially during the most severe cold and when it snowed; for it was then the smoke assailed us with the greatest fury"

A hundred yards offshore, the cedarstrip passed by. Slow but steady, that old canoe that had carried the father as a child now carried the children of the father. Would it mean as much to his son and daughter as it meant to him? The idea of owning a canoe and passing it down to my children and they to theirs and so on appealed to me. Long after I was gone, it would still be Dad's canoe, or Grandpa's or even Great-Grandpa's, and in that way, I could still be around to share with them the joy of paddling the lakes and rivers that had meant so much to me.

Canoes are simple, unassuming craft. There is nothing superfluous in their design. They go about their business quietly, without pretense of being anything other than what they are. Rugged strength lies within their graceful symmetry. They can bear heavy burdens. If capsized in rough waters, they will not sink. They foster lasting friendships and bestow upon the traveller the privilege of engaging in an ancient process that reveals more than just the country of the journey. They provide the stage for an elevated sense of sight and smell and sound and touch and thought. They are the key for entry into a realm of enchantment. Canoes, in fact, are the spirits of saints. Former prime minister Pierre Elliot Trudeau, a canoeist himself, wrote, "What sets a canoeing expedition apart is that it purifies you more rapidly and inescapably than any other. Travel a thousand miles by train and you are a brute; pedal 500 miles on a bicycle and you remain basically a bourgeois; paddle 100 miles in a canoe and you are already a child of nature."

I closed the book again at the page where I'd opened it. In the humidity, my brain had shut down. It was a struggle just to think about getting up to start supper. How had Lawrence, an Englishman, functioned so energetically in the heart of Arabia? It would occur to me later that the very attributes that had served the Jesuits in this land — a good education, toughness in adversity, exceptional perseverance, passionate pursuit of a goal — would be recognized three centuries later in T.E. Lawrence during his First World War campaigns in the Arabian desert. The qualities that drive men in religion and war grow from common ground.

I fanned the smouldering fire with the frying pan. The heavy, dead air made for slow combustion. Supper was Kraft Dinner. Suzanne put Barbie back in the tent as I spooned out the macaroni into the bowls and filled the pot with water to let it soak.

"What should we do after supper?" I said.

She surprised me by saying we could go for a hike. I thought for sure it would be another swim, which would have suited me fine. Hiking through the woods late on a hot afternoon and kicking up mosquitos from the underbrush was not on my agenda.

"OK, but first why don't we go for a swim to cool off."

The lake had flattened out, and once again dark clouds crowded the horizon. A cool rain would have been welcome — almost. My enjoyment of rain on a canoe trip comes when the tent is up and I'm lying inside, listening to its tattoo on the roof. Rain beating on the roof while I lie cocooned in my sleeping bag is a powerful sedative. Nowadays, there are all kinds of YouTube sites with this very soundtrack. But if I have ever enjoyed a downpour while out on a lake or traversing a portage, I've forgotten it. On a portage, rain beating against the canoe hull drains down the hull's sides, runs along the gunnels until it reaches your hands, then pours down the sleeves of your rain jacket to collect at the elbows in cold pools. You laugh about it afterward, but *bonhomie* would not describe your frame of mind at the time. As for being out on a lake in thunder and lightning, it's best not to tempt Mother Nature. Go ashore, where a lightning strike is less likely to find you, and wait until the storm passes.

So far, the weather had cooperated, and I suspected the clouds to the west just might break up and disappear as they had the night before. They were like a black dog that was all bark and no bite, a kind of benign threat that nevertheless kept you guessing. The higher elevation of this section of the park seemed to be acting as a fence, keeping it at bay. We sat eating our KD and looking at the lake.

It is pleasant just to sit and look at a lake in Algonquin, especially toward sundown with the softer light on the trees and rocks reflecting quiet images. The feathery green needles and sweeping boughs of the white pine and the shoreline grasses paint a delicate picture on the liquid canvas, something like Monet might have captured had he come this way. To the observer, the advantage of nature's brush is that its paintings are never finished, but changing continually with the mood and colour of the water.

There is a quality about water that allows us to sit patiently beside it for long periods of time, content simply to be in its presence. It kneads the tensions of civilized life, and the canoe tripper, being on it, in it or camped beside it for days on end, succumbs to its healing magic. Water travel imposes its languid pace. We are forced to slow down, and in the physical deceleration, the peaks and valleys of our life begin to level out. At day's end, the reward is weary contentment and a cheerful campfire.

Canoe tripping is mind altering. In the span of human evolution, our ability to move faster than our own two legs can carry us is barely measurable and is punctuated by a skyrocketing spike on this end of the graph. In the wake of our technological victories, where we can find ourselves spiritually adrift, canoeing is a route to our ancestral past. Paddling day after day, unhurried, methodical, waterborne, we seep unconsciously into the crevices of our origins where enchantment with the world was our daily bread. We are enlightened with feelings of well-being and achievement and a sense that we have tapped into something beyond the physical boundaries of our journey. "A lake is the landscape's most beautiful and expressive feature," wrote Thoreau. "It is the earth's eye; looking into which the beholder measures the depth of his own nature."

"When are we going home?" Suzanne asked. Her question surprised me.

"In a few days. We camp three more nights." I peeled back the lid on an applesauce tin and handed her the dessert.

"Would you like to go home?" I wondered if she was feeling homesick.

"No." She shook her head.

I wasn't convinced. This was the first time she had been cut off from the rest of her family for more than a day.

"We're not going home anyway, remember? We have to go to Nana's first. Mummy and Laurie are at Nana's house."

"Are we staying at Nana's too?"

"We'll be there for a whole week, then I have to go back to work."

"Why do you have to work all the time?"

"So we can have holidays and go on canoe trips like this." She contemplated this for a moment.

"If you didn't go to work we could go on holidays every day."

"Well, maybe." This logic was clear to her and I let it go at that.

I sunk the bowls and spoons into the water in the pot. It was beginning to steam, plenty hot for dishwashing. I took the pot off the grill, added some cold and gave Suzanne the soap and dishcloth.

"You clean up and I'll try to find a better tree for our pack."

We were in the western half of the park where the soil is mainly glacial till, which favours hardwood growth. There were plenty of birch and sugar maple and a scattering of red oak, but nothing I could see to suit the purpose at hand. I made a short circuit through the woods without losing sight of Suzanne and returned to look again at our lone pine. The branch was long enough, but I was sure it would snap if I tried to sling the pack farther out from the trunk. The cans of food added too much weight, and I hadn't helped the problem by bringing a little extra, just in case. After our swim, we would go for a paddle and take the pack with us. Somewhere nearby there was bound to be a tree to run it up.

The refreshing coolness of the lake was a balm. The depth dropped off quickly from the campsite, but there was a small knee-deep area where Suzanne could splash around. I floated on my back, keeping my eye on her. She was on her hands and knees, her face inches above the water. Something seemed to have caught her attention. I was about to ask her what she'd found when she dunked her head, then came up sputtering and wiping her eyes.

"Good for you! See! You can do it! Take a big breath and try again. See how long you can stay under."

She took a big breath, puffed out her cheeks and went under for a count of two, came up and flashed a smile. A breakthrough. She ducked a couple more times, blowing bubbles on the last try. It had been a slow road getting to this point, but finally she had taken the plunge. Her swimming lessons should start showing progress. I floated over and gave her a pat on the back, telling her how proud of her I was.

When you eyeball a lake from surface level, it's a bit like looking through a wide-angle lens. You have a vision of panoramic proportions. From this low viewpoint, I could see no other human activity, but a couple of canoes had pulled in at our previous site directly across the lake. The campsite next to it was also occupied, and a trail of blue smoke filtered through the treetops. They had best prepare for a late-night guest. There was no reason to believe we had been privileged and that the bear over there would not be around to check them out too. I wondered if the pack-slashing bear at our site had had any luck with the previous campers who bivouacked here. Maybe that was why it had been reluctant to leave. Maybe the pickings the night before had been good. Campers who don't properly cache their food are a menace to themselves and to those who follow. Their bad habits teach bears to associate humans with fast food, and eventually the animal can become emboldened to the point where confronting it with a paddle and a shout are a big mistake.

We changed into our clothes that I'd hung out to air on a clothesline tied between two trees, put the pack and rope into the canoe and shoved off. It was seven o'clock, which gave us plenty of time to do some exploring. Instead of going back to the marsh we had passed earlier, I went around the point just to the west of our site and then into a long arm of the lake running east. The water was calm and the canoe slid across its surface. It was a dream to paddle, the dark reflections of the trees bending around the silver rims of the whorls and spinning down into them, then water rushing to fill them up and flatten out again.

Suzanne sat in the bow seat with her hands on the gunnels, watching the trees drift by. She seemed to have forgotten her idea of a hike. There are hiking trails in Algonquin, but the park's interior definitely revolves around the canoe. In a country studded with beautiful lakes, the canoe is freedom, allowing you to go anywhere. Hiking is nice, but it cramps your freedom, confining you to narrow trails and shorelines. One of the enjoyable pleasures of the park is doing exactly what we were doing, taking a leisurely cruise on a soft summer evening.

I kept to the shore and the cooling forest shadows. The opposite shore remained sunlit, and I could see someone in a red shirt who appeared to be fishing. We passed a campsite with bathing suits strung on a line, but neither canoe nor tent to be seen. Near the tip of the arm where there was shallower water, a great blue heron took flight, coasted off a little way and landed to resume its watch for frogs and fish. These huge birds range throughout the park and you can usually count on a sighting or two. They keep their distance, but do not seem to be overly alarmed by humans. On the long, winding creek through the marsh between Proulx and Little Crow Lakes, north of Opeongo, I have watched a great blue take off and land ahead of us several times before finally circling around to head back the way we'd come, content that it had lured us away from its favourite fishing spot.

I lay the paddle across the gunnels. The canoe slowed and came to rest in a swath of water lilies. We sat there taking in the view, scarcely hearing so much as a birdcall. I lifted the binoculars. Water and trees, shadow and light. I closed with the zoom, the distance of ten football fields compressing to one in the blink of an eye. In the concentrated field, details of rocks and tree bark and sunlit leaves seemed close enough to touch.

"Can I look?" Suzanne said.

I set the binoculars on the paddle blade and passed them to her, telling her to put the strap around her neck.

"See if you can see where the heron landed."

Her delicate fingers gripped the binoculars as she tried to hold them steady. It would have made a nice photo. I saw her framed against the background of soft greens with the lake to her right and the bow end of the canoe visible to her left, a subtle hint of a wilderness adventure. It was the kind of scene I would see in Canadian artist Yvette Miller's family outdoors paintings two decades later, captured with a grace beyond the realm of any camera.

"See anything?"

"A duck."

"Are you sure it's a duck and not a loon?"

She raised the binoculars again.

"It's a duck," she said.

I paddled into the light and headed back along the north shore. On this side of the arm, the air was warm. Suzanne kept lifting the binoculars to her eyes.

"There's a man in the water with a red shirt," she said as we passed a tiny island tucked close to the mainland.

"What's he doing?"

There was a long pause.

"Fishing."

I paddled slowly, and slowly the detail of the fisherman became delineated. The shirt was red plaid, and he wore a cap and beige waders up to his waist with his shirt tucked inside. He was casting with the rod and reeling in, the sun catching the wet line in sparks of light. He didn't notice our approach until we were very close.

"Hello!" he said

I returned the greeting.

"Beautiful evening. Looking for a site?"

The pack was in the canoe. I said that we were camped at the next site around the point. I waited for him to finish reeling in the lure so I could paddle past.

A woman came through the trees, her hand in an oven mitt. She waved to us.

"I thought I heard voices!" she said. Her smile filled her round face and crinkled her eyes.

"Sometimes my husband talks to himself," she laughed. "I wasn't sure."

The fishing line flashed again. It didn't look like he'd caught anything.

"Are you enjoying your holiday, dear?" the woman asked Suzanne. Suzanne nodded.

"They're our neighbours," her husband said. "The site around the point."

"Is this your first time in the park?" the woman said.

It was Suzanne's first trip, I said. She was a big woman in height and weight. Her grey hair was clipped short, which made her round face look even rounder.

"Uh, oh."

I looked back at the fisherman. His line had gone taut.

"Snagged on something," he said. He tugged on the line, swinging the rod left and right. "Got 'er good this time."

I paddled to where the line disappeared into the water.

"Give it some slack," I said. "Maybe I can free it from here."

I brought the line to me with the paddle and carefully pulled on it. The lure easily broke free.

"Great! Thanks. One of my favourite spinners. I'd hate to lose it."

"Can you join us for coffee?" the woman asked. "I've just taken the pot off the fire." She showed us her mitt. "Lloyd was going to catch some fish to have with the biscuits I made, but I think it'll just be biscuits, won't it Lloyd?" Her eyes crinkled up.

"They'll still be warm," Lloyd said. "We've got butter and strawberry jam to go with them."

Campfire biscuits and butter and strawberry jam — I beached the canoe. Grace introduced herself and we followed her back to the fire. Places were set for two, including two aluminum chairs with armrests. I apologized for interrupting their dinner.

"No, no," Lloyd said. "We had dinner three hours ago. This is snack time."

He took the top off the pot he'd pulled from the lake as he waded out and reached in to retrieve a chunk of butter wrapped in saran wrap. Suzanne and I sat on the log next to the chairs. The site was very tidy. The space around the firepit was swept clean to hard ground, the firepit rocks fitted to allow the grill to rest perfectly flat on top. The tent was blue with a red fly and big enough to stand in. Two guy lines at each corner pulled the material smooth. Lloyd rested his fishing rod against a tree and sat down.

"We set up here four days ago," he said. "It took two days to get here and it's about as far as we go anymore. Getting too old for this kind of thing I'm afraid. As long as we don't overdo it we've still got a few years left to enjoy it."

He nodded toward the lake. The sun was still above the distant treeline, filling the site with ragged patches of yellow light. It gave promise of a beautiful sunset and a good day tomorrow.

"We started bringing our kids up here when they were around your daughter's age, and then our grandchildren," he went on. "But now they're grown too, so we're in a bit of a holding pattern until our great-grandchildren are old enough."

He chuckled at the thought. I could scarcely believe they were great-grandparents. It made me feel good about my own canoeing prospects. Grace handed me a cup and poured the coffee, and then gave Suzanne a small cardboard juice box with a straw in it. The warm golden brown biscuits smothered in butter and jam were a piece of heaven dropped down to earth.

"Our first trip up here was what, Grace, 1926?"

"That was our first trip together," she said. "I was up twice before, with my parents and sisters. We stayed at Minnesing."

"Minnesing!" I said. "Where the chimneys are still standing?"

"Yes. You saw those, did you? We'd sit by one of those fireplaces most evenings, reading, playing cards, talking. We got there by horse and cart from the Cache Lake train station. It was ten miles of bumpy road from there to the lodge, a dreadful ride. We walked more than we rode."

"What kinds of activities were there?" I said, amazed to be talking to someone who had actually been a guest at the lodge.

"The same as what we do now in the park. Canoeing, hiking, swimming, sailing. My father taught biology at the University of Toronto. He loved the park, God rest his soul. Going on a hike with him was a learning adventure. He gave my sisters and me an indelible appreciation of nature and Algonquin."

She turned to Suzanne. "You're very lucky to have a father who brings you here, Suzanne. What do you like best about Algonquin Park so far?"

"Swimming."

"Are you a good swimmer?"

"My Dad is teaching me how to float."

"Have you seen any animals?"

She nodded. "A beaver and a bear."

"A beaver and a bear! My goodness! Where did you see the bear?"

"It was beside the tent licking orange juice."

I gave them a rundown of our encounter.

"We've seen our share of them over the years, haven't we Lloyd. But I can't say we ever had a problem except the night one climbed into our canoe."

Lloyd slouched in his chair, his suspenders peeled from his shoulders, a grin on his face as he remembered. But he shook his head ever so slightly, glancing at Suzanne. He did not want to chance alarming her with the story. I steered the conversation back to the lodge.

"You must have been sorry to see Minnesing torn down," I said.

"Oh my, it was a shock! We hadn't been on Burnt Island for three or four years. Then we come back and just the chimneys left. I don't think I truly realized what it meant to me until it was gone. A lot of memories. I'm sure most people who pass the place now have no idea what it once was."

We got onto the subject of canoe routes, and like most people who frequent the park, found that we had been to many of the same places. Where I had not been was the Barron River, which Lloyd assured me I would enjoy. He showed me on his map where it was on the park's eastern boundary. Part of its course lies between three-hundred-foot-high cliffs through which the Upper Great Lakes once drained. It's spotted with picturesque waterfalls. At the highest falls, there is a granite chute you can slide down, the river rushing down and pushing you forcefully straight into a huge circular granite pool. My Barron River trip still lay twenty years into the future and I would go there with family and friends more than once, and as Lloyd predicted, we had a whale of a time!

I had a little more coffee and split the last biscuit with him. His canoe was a cedarstrip-and-canvas model, a Chestnut Prospector. If I could have any canoe I wanted, it's the one I'd pick. His children had it specially made and presented it to him as a retirement gift. It was red with thin brass bumper trim protecting the bow and stern. The gunnels, thwarts and yoke were mahogany, the seats rawhide webbing in mahogany frames, all of which were rubbed down with tung oil, which he applied every spring and fall. He didn't use varnish, as it tended to crack, allowing water to seep underneath and over time damage the wood. Tung oil was the best protection.

"It was a total surprise," he said, laughing. "I had no idea they were getting me anything. I've made it clear that I'm to be buried with it. There may be canoeing in the happy hunting ground."

The Chestnut was sixteen feet long and weighed seventy-two pounds, the same as mine. But that was the extent of the similarity. Anything further would be like measuring the qualities of a windowpane in your house to the stained-glass glory of a European cathedral. For that matter, even the weight was pushing it. A seventy-two-pound cedarstrip-and-canvas Chestnut is not as heavy as seventy-two pounds of moulded fibreglass. On the weigh scale, the numbers will read the same, but on the shoulders over a portage there is a buoyancy, almost a life, to the Chestnut that deadweight fibreglass cannot duplicate.

The Prospector was the canoe of choice for the man who has been called "the patron saint of canoeing," renowned Canadian wilderness canoeist, author and filmmaker Bill Mason, and it goes without saying that his esteem for the Prospector influenced my own thinking about these craft. Over the course of his life, Mason received many honours, including his portrait on a Canadian postage stamp. The Chestnut that he considered his favourite is on display in Peterborough, Ontario, at the Canadian Canoe Museum, the world's largest collection of canoes, kayaks and paddled watercraft. When he said the canoe was one of the greatest inventions of mankind, he wasn't kidding. "There is nothing," he said, "that is so aesthetically pleasing and yet so functional and versatile as the canoe." He believed that God had created the canoe first, then invented Canada for a place to paddle it. Such is the role of the canoe in Canada's history that the federal, provincial and municipal governments have invested $14.4 million toward the construction of a new forty-nine-thousand-square-foot Canadian Canoe Museum at another Peterborough site.

Among Mason's many wilderness canoe trips, the South Nahanni River in the Northwest Territories stands out for its Virginia Falls, which tumble down from a height near twice that of Niagara. At the base of the falls, a massive rock spire rises from the tumult. When he died of cancer in 1988 at the age of fifty-nine, it was suggested that the spire be named after him. It has become widely known among serious canoeists as Mason's Rock. His award-winning films can be seen for free on the National Film Board's website.

Grace put a few sticks on the fire. In the intense heat of the coals, they ignited at once, the flames licking up through the grill. Lloyd yawned, his empty cup dangling from his finger.

"I can't be tired," he said. "I slept half the afternoon."

"We tend to nap quite a bit nowadays," Grace said. "There was a time when we'd go from Canoe Lake to Big Trout in a day, wasn't there, dear?"

Lloyd shook his head. "There was, and I find it hard to believe. Just getting to the north end of Canoe Lake is the big achievement now."

She patted him on the shoulder and took his cup. Suzanne sat staring droopy eyed at the fire. I thanked them for their hospitality. It was time we headed back to camp. Tomorrow should be a good day, Lloyd said, looking west. He walked into the water in his boots and steadied the canoe while Suzanne and I got in.

"Here, Lloyd," said Grace, "give this to Suzanne."

Lloyd handed Suzanne a small package and gently pushed us off into the lake.

"Have fun the rest of your trip," Grace called after us.

We waved and left them standing on the shore, and when I looked back after a minute or two, they were still there watching after us.

8

*When children come into contact
with nature, they reveal their strengths.*

− Maria Montessori

We coasted around the point. The lake lay empty and serene, the soft evening light painting it in pastel hues. Over half a century ago, Grace would have seen evenings like this from the veranda of Minnesing with her sisters and mother and father. And now only the chimneys, columns of pale stone reaching into the sky like the ruins of a lost civilization. We would stop on the way home and look around. Grace had breathed life into the place and piqued my interest.

"What did Grace give you?" I asked, curious.

"Cookies."

"Is one of them for me do you think?"

"Yep."

In the royal blue sea of sky six miles straight up, the shark outline of a jetliner lit by the setting sun headed east, the distant thunder of its engines a reminder of that other world beyond the boundaries of our Eden. To this day, I am still struck by the contrast when I look up from my seat in a canoe on a wilderness lake to see a mode of travel scarcely dreamed of when Grace and Lloyd were children like

Suzanne. From paddle to jet fuel in scarcely more than a century, from grinding labour for the gain of a few miles a day to five hundred miles per hour and "a gin and tonic please." It is a stupendous leap, yet we acknowledge it simply as a natural progression of our journey on earth. Algonquin gives us the opportunity to think about the journey and its destination by allowing us to change frequency, like turning the dial on the radio to filter out the clamour of urban life and tune in to the sounds of wind and water, birdsong, solitude and silence. Recordings of nature's sounds, often to the accompaniment of soothing music, is recognition of something amiss in the human spirit.

In the introduction to his 1981 book *The Re-enchantment of the World*, Morris Berman wrote, "For more than ninety-nine percent of human history the world was enchanted and man saw himself as an integral part of it. The complete reversal of this perception in a mere four hundred years or so has destroyed the continuity of the human experience and the integrity of the human psyche."

We are not superior to our past. In the pursuit of making a living, we need to take the time to find a quiet place and listen to its voice. In doing so, we will have rendered a kindness to our children and the planet.

We bumped ashore. I helped Suzanne out to keep her feet dry and hoisted the pack out of the canoe.

"You can have a cookie, then get your pyjamas on and brush your teeth."

I put the rest of the cookies in the pack and ran it back up the pine tree, but without the cans. The lighter weight permitted me the extension I needed on the branch to hang the pack far enough from the trunk. In a stroke of ingenuity, I had decided that the cans could go on a rock ledge that lay under two feet of water, just to the left of the campsite. If the bear returned, it wouldn't see or smell them down there or even think to look for them in the water.

    I surveyed the site. Everything looked to be shipshape. The only thing left to do in the remaining light was prepare the firepit. I scraped away the warm ash and sprinkled water on it to eliminate any chance of an unplanned rekindling, and erected a log cabin of sticks on top of some birchbark and the labels I'd peeled from the cans before sinking them. I could tell more or less what they contained by their relative sizes. Then, for insurance, some brown pine needles and a length of toilet paper. Above this I positioned larger sticks so that they fanned out around the whole in a teepee shape, much like we'd built for Barbie earlier. At the apex, a dead pine bough with a fan of brown needles that would ignite like kerosene and draw the fire into a blaze. Over all this and the extra wood piled beside the firepit, I carefully spread the groundsheet to prevent any dampening by the moist night air. If I needed a fire on a moment's notice, this would do it. I straightened up and felt my pockets to make sure I knew where to reach for the matches.

    Suzanne had pulled on her pyjamas and was at the shore with her toothbrush, looking across the lake, when suddenly she turned and came over to me and without saying a word raised her arms. I picked her up. She put her arms around my neck and her head on my shoulder. I stood holding her and patting her on the back, rocking gently. For three days we had been each other's sole companion in these woods far from home and family, and I now suddenly realized I could not remember having given her a hug or a kiss or told her that I loved her. Engrossed in our activities and getting from here to there, I had neglected the most important part of any parent-child relationship, and in her simple, unspoken gesture I was humbled.

"You've had a busy day," I said, setting her down after a bit. We got our life jackets and sat on them, side by side at the water's edge, she leaning against me, and watched the western horizon fade from pink to green. A soft, warm breeze flowed around us.

"What was your favourite thing you did today?" I said.

She thought for a moment and said, "Swimming at the beach."

"Tomorrow we can have another swimming lesson. You can try floating again."

"I put my face in the water!"

"I know, and if you can do that and float at the same time like I showed you, you'll be swimming in no time."

What was it that had suddenly given Suzanne the courage to put her face in the water? You know instinctively you won't be able to breathe. It can be a scary thing the first time. Might her newfound daring have had something to do with her new environment? Travelling on large bodies of water and sleeping next to them day in and day out diminish their intimidation. Things like ashes in your stew or an ant floating in your cup that would give you the heebie-jeebies back home don't faze you when you're sitting on a log beside a campfire in the depths of the forest. Paddling lakes and living in the bush give you the opportunity to see things from a different perspective.

Time would come after my children had grown, when I would learn about the contributions made to childhood education by physician and educator Dr. Maria Montessori. She would have been a big fan of canoe trips for kids. She believed, as is generally accepted today, that the first five or six years of a child's education are crucial. To that end, she maintained their education should focus more on the natural processes that develop spontaneously rather than focus on what the teacher says and does. A child's early education is less about listening to words and more about the interaction of the child with his or her environment. Children in their earliest years, she said, are capable of tremendous achievements through the *unconscious* power of absorption. Her book *The Absorbent Mind* remains a cornerstone to her teachings.

The first Montessori school opened in a low-income district in Rome in 1907, and in North America her philosophy of education received the early support of influential people like Thomas Edison and Alexander Graham Bell. Today, Montessori schools can be found in countries around the world. Montessori pupils learn by doing, by developing their cognitive powers through direct experience: touching, seeing, hearing, tasting, smelling and moving. That sounds a lot like the great outdoors to me. Impressions don't merely enter a child's mind, she said, they form it. For me, impressions received in the embrace of nature rank among the best.

I flicked a pebble into the water. On the opposite shore, a spot of light flickered from our site of the night before, the campfire of its new tenants. I pointed it out to Suzanne. Pot banging and yelling from over there tonight would not surprise me. Your first thought when you hear that kind of ruckus from afar is "I'm glad it's not us," which is quickly followed by "Are we next?"

"When Mummy and Laurie see the movie, they'll wish they came with us," I said.

"They can come next time."

I said they would, and was about to add that I would take some film of her doing her float, when I remembered that there was none. I would kick myself about this for a long time. I flicked another pebble and watched the tiny rings radiate across the surface.

"Would you like to come back to Algonquin Park next summer?"

She nodded. "Yep. If we camp here Mummy and Laurie could see the bear."

"Yes, maybe they could. We'd have to do a better job of hanging up our food."

More people would mean more food and more weight. An extra pack and a second rope would be needed. Unless the branch was a hefty one, you'd need to spread the weight by running half of it up a second tree. In the years ahead, when I would travel with larger groups, more than one food pack hanging high was the norm.

"It'll be dark pretty soon," I said, "and you still haven't brushed your teeth." She put some water in a cup, and with a dab of toothpaste on her brush, swished it around. "When you're done it's time to get into your sleeping bag. I'll be in in a few minutes. And close the tent so the mosquitos don't get in."

When she was done, I heard the tent zipped up then down and a rustling around as she wiggled into her sleeping bag. I pulled my pipe from the zip pocket on my clothes pack. I'm not a smoker, but I made canoe trips the exception. On canoe trips the pipe is an essential part of my gear, just as it had been for the voyageurs. They would measure distances in pipes. It was common practice for them to lay down their paddles for a few minutes each hour or so to rest and enjoy a smoke, and then at day's end to recall how many pipes they had travelled. It was a simple pleasure that helped make their gruelling eighteen-hour day tolerable. My pipe was a link to that colourful era of Canadian history. Filling the bowl, tamping it, the strike and flare of the match, the smell of sulphur, the flame sucked down into the *tabac*, the sweet aroma, the smoke curling away, the expanding warmth of the polished briar in the palm. At twilight on a woodland shore, these simple elements were a near mystical ritual, conjuring exploits from a time when daring and self-reliance were a steady diet for *les hommes*.

In his *Narrative of Explorations in Western America*, which cover the period from 1807 to 1832, map-maker David Thompson recorded a fatal example of the kind of hazards the voyageurs experienced: "They preferred running the Dalles; they had not gone far, when to avoid the ridge of waves, which they ought to have kept, they took the apparent smooth water, were drawn into a whirlpool, which wheeled them around into its Vortex: the canoe with the men clinging to it, went down end foremost, and all were drowned; at the foot of the Dalles search was made for their bodies but only one man was found, his body much mangled by the rocks."

During his long career with the Hudson's Bay Company, David Thompson travelled some sixty thousand miles and mapped nearly three million square miles of territory. Famed geologist J.B. Tyrell considered Thompson to be "the greatest practical land geographer the world has produced." As a member of the Geological Survey of Canada at the tail end of the nineteenth century, Tyrell travelled on horseback, by canoe and on foot over much of the same territory covered by Thompson three-quarters of a century earlier. Thompson died in near obscurity in Montreal in 1857, but Tyrell would work tirelessly and with great success to establish the man's reputation and his work in the eyes of the public. He saw to the publication of dozens of Thompson's notebooks, and in partnership with the Canadian Historical Society, placed a marker at Thompson's unmarked Montreal gravesite. The David Thompson Highway in Alberta, the Thompson River in British Columbia and Thompson Falls in Montana are among the many honours bestowed on the man on both sides of the 49th parallel. When Thompson died, he had been married for fifty-eight years to Charlotte Small, the daughter of a Scottish fur trader and a Cree mother. There is a bronze statue of Thompson and Charlotte in the town of Invermere, British Columbia. Despite their family of thirteen children, Charlotte managed to accompany her husband on many of his wilderness journeys.

The unmistakable thump of paddle against gunnel broke my reverie, then a girl saying she smelled pipe tobacco and this site must be taken too. I stood up. There were four canoes, obviously from a girls' camp, and I got a few feeble hellos as they slid past twenty feet away. I was surprised that they were still on the go at this hour. In another ten minutes they would need flashlights to see the shore. I called out to the counsellor in the second canoe.

"There's some space here. You're welcome to it."

She thanked me and said they'd keep looking, that there was bound to be something up ahead. Actually, there was not much space at our site at all, but I had done the hospitable thing. Afloat on a dark lake with a clutch of young girls was a big and probably worrying responsibility. Had Suzanne been sitting beside me, perhaps they would have been amenable to my offer. I told her not to go into the arm, that the sites there were all occupied too. Considering the time, they had probably gotten a late start out of Big Trout six portages back. I watched them fade quickly into the dusk in the direction of the chimneys. Minnesing was not a designated site, but there would be enough space there for their tents if they had reached the end of their rope.

Writing the paragraph above jogs my memory about a young woman our canoe party met one summer as she arrived at our end of a portage somewhere in the park's Lake Louisa sector. She looked to be in her midtwenties, and when we asked how many people she was travelling with, she answered in accented English that she was on her own. She had flown from Germany, rented a car in Toronto and her gear from a local outfitter, got her map and headed out. She had never been on a canoe trip in her life, but it was something she had always wanted to do, so she did it. Needless to say, we were impressed by her resolve. But that's the kind of thing you can do in Algonquin and feel comfortable about it. I have been paddling the park for nearly fifty years, and bears aside, I have always felt entirely comfortable in its setting.

9

A Pooh Bear takes care of his tummy by never forgetting to eat.

- Winnie the Pooh

I opened my eyes. The tent pitch black. No mistake about what had disturbed my uneasy sleep. It was back. The approaching thump-thump-thump, the vibrations, then the breathing. The breathing is the most unnerving. It gives a heart-pumping proximity to the bear that is as real as imagined. It came straight for the tent. Was it the same bear or another bear, a bigger bear? My stomach muscles knotted into a ball. Had Suzanne brought some of Grace's cookies to bed with her? I pulled my arms out of the sleeping bag. If it slashed through the tent the way it had through the pack, we were in trouble. Instinctively I reached for Suzanne, ready to pull her toward me. It was a futile gesture. If the animal was coming in, we had no defence. One of its paws caught the rear guy line with a twang, shaking the tent, then loud snuffling up against the tent wall.

    I could yell. It might be scared off. On the other hand, it might not. It might be startled and turn aggressive. If I let out a yell, it would certainly frighten Suzanne who was sleeping through the whole business like a baby.

Suddenly the bear found something and ripped into it. I was at a loss. Everything had gone up the tree. What could I have forgotten? It moved a few paces away and continued to thrash whatever it had found. I waited, wanting to look out the porthole, but not daring to move. The luminous hands on my watch read ten minutes to eleven.

The thrashing stopped. The bear shuffled past the front of the tent. The pots I had left at the back of the firepit rattled. I wondered if it would shred the dishcloth because of its smell. I got to my knees and lifted the porthole flap. The bear was blacker than the night. I could see its silhouette plainly against the backdrop of the moonlit lake as it went to the pine tree, and without pausing climbed with surprising agility up to the branch. But this time the pack was out of reach. There would be no more free snacks. It would have to look elsewhere. There were plenty of other campsites it could follow its nose to — not a neighbourly thought, but we didn't need its undivided attention. It clung to the trunk like grim death, reluctant to accept defeat with the prize so tantalizingly close. But there was no option except to creep out on the branch, and it knew enough not to try. The branch would have snapped like a twig. It came back down and wandered off toward the canoe.

I retrieved the matches I'd tucked away in the corner of the tent. It would take me five seconds to get out of the tent, yank the groundsheet off the firepit and ignite the toilet paper stuffed inside my carefully prepared log cabin. Ten seconds more and I would have a blaze. Our visitor would skedaddle.

As I started cautiously to unzip the tent, the bear went into the water, not just a splish-splash like last night, but a plunge worthy of a belly flop off a diving board. In a moment it was out again, and

I heard the dull thud of a can hitting a rock. So much for my clever idea. I'd been outsmarted. So quickly had it found the cans that I wondered if it had been watching from the bushes while I was "hiding" them. I heard it bite through the metal and slurp the contents. What to do? There would be no repeat in the dead of night of my matinee performance, especially with it dining on Irish stew or butterscotch pudding. The fire was the only answer. If I didn't scare it off, it would rip open every can. Another plunge, and this time it came out of the water toward the tent, wheezing from exertion. Past the tent and up the slope behind. Silence. I waited. What next?

Suzanne sighed, safe in her dreams. She hadn't moved a muscle. I looked out the back porthole. Maybe it had left. Then the sound of teeth puncturing metal again, and a can bouncing down the slope toward the tent. I froze. The bear came down right behind and snagged it from where it had stopped against the tent wall. It clanked between the bear's teeth, six inches from my head. I had to light the fire. It went wheezing back up the slope. Silence. I slowly unzipped the tent and crawled out, trying to see into the dark. The night air was cool and damp, the moon on the water a ghostly sheen. I took the matchbox from my pocket and placed the ends of two matches between my lips. The stillness was ethereal. Where was my adversary? I slowly got to my feet, and crouching low as if to make myself invisible to the bear, crept to the firepit. The match flared. Night became day in a cauldron of flame.

I stood as close to the fire as I could without scorching myself and looked quickly around. I had clear vision for fifty feet. Suzanne's red pack lay on the ground. I had left it beside the tent. It was empty, but the bear must have smelled our lunchtime tuna sandwiches. No wonder our furry poacher had pounced on it. The light reflected off the canoe, and behind it I could see the shoreline where I had submerged the cans. Nothing there. I scanned through the trees and along the crest of the slope, and there the bear sat, doglike again, bathed in firelight, water droplets glistening on its fur. A can lay between its front paws, the large can that I recognized as the pork and beans. As we looked at each other, it got to all fours, looked to either side, sniffed the ground once, picked up the can in its teeth, turned and vanished.

I kept the fire going, poking at it with a stick whenever it started to die down, my shadow dancing around the campsite like a crazed giant jumping on the tent and the canoe, shooting up tree trunks and into the canopy of leaves, the flames and the twisting giant enough to make any bear turn tail. As the minutes passed and there was no more sign of our visitor, I could feel myself relaxing and breathing easier. It had been tense. I shudder to think what might have happened had Suzanne's tuna-smelling pack been inside with us, but the bear's response was a salient reminder of my Rule Number 1: Never bring food into the tent.

Years later, from about the early 1990s onward, I have canoed Algonquin every summer and not once has a bear showed up at my campsite. Two changes have made a positive difference since the early seventies when I was there with Suzanne: a 1978 ban on carrying cans and bottles into the park interior and campers who are better educated about respecting the environment. No garbage is left behind, at least not by responsible campers, who are by far the majority. It is either burned or packed out. This in turn has educated the bears. As an animal that runs on its stomach, it has learned that there is little point to a campsite visit. There's food, but it is always out of reach. This is not to say that a visit will never happen, but in my personal experience over the past decades, those exciting nocturnal encounters of an earlier time have pretty much become a thing of the past.

In the light of the fire, I walked around the site. A butterscotch pudding tin lay near the canoe, full of bullet-like holes and empty. There were still some cans on the underwater ledge. We seemed to have gotten off without too much damage. I swished the pudding tin in the lake and placed it with the pots.

There was a chill to the night, and the warmth and glow of the fire was comforting. Sparks rose on the heated air, and through the openings in the trees I could see a scattering of stars, their glitter subdued by the round, white moon. The past twenty-four hours had been eventful. If I could get another few hours of uninterrupted sleep, I'd feel ready for another day. In preparing for the trip, I hadn't taken into consideration or even understood how around-the-clock responsibility for a five-year-old in a wilderness environment can wear you out. My unintended nap on the first day was typical of other trips, but on this trip, there was no place for the indulgence.

I kept the fire burning brightly for an hour, occasionally walking around it to let the bear know I was still on guard, and when my eyelids finally grew too heavy, I crawled back into the tent. In the faint firelight filtering through the canvas, I could see Suzanne's hair, the rest of her hidden away in her sleeping bag. She hadn't moved. I zipped myself back into my own bag and rolled on my side. When I opened my eyes again, the sun was up with a pair of blue jays in full screeching voice.

We took our time breaking camp. It was a sunny morning, but with more cottonball clouds than we'd seen the last couple of days. The wind was out of the west and had stirred a bit of a chop on the lake. I folded the tent in three sections and rolled it up, brushing off the pine needles and dirt and daddy-long-legs.

"Can you get the cans out of the water?" I said. "We don't want to forget them." The remaining cans lay submerged and untouched.

Suzanne trotted off to have a look.

"I can't get them," she said, squatting and running her hands through the water.

"Put on your bathing suit, then you can reach them."

It was all she needed to hear. I stuffed the tent into its sack, along with the poles and pegs, and tied it closed while Suzanne stripped and pulled on her bikini. We would head west. We had a couple of nights left, and hopefully we could spend them without Mr. Bruin. It was unlikely he would forget the cans in the water. There would probably be another visit tonight. Anybody who might camp here would have an excellent chance of seeing one of the park's more prominent residents up close.

Suzanne retrieved the cans and set them on the ground. "Can I try to float?"

"Sure."

She was standing knee-deep. She put her head between her arms, bent at the waist, hesitated, then fell forward. The float lasted all of a second or two before she was up sputtering and wiping the hair from her eyes.

"Hooray! You did it! That was great!"

She grinned and tried again, this time managing a fraction longer.

"OK, now try it while kicking your feet."

She did this, advancing the length of her arms.

"Excellent. Now you're learning to swim."

She nodded, pleased with herself. A milestone had been reached. After two years in lakes and swimming pools, trying to get her to that goal, it was done in the blink of an eye. This phase of my coaching job was over. Dogged perseverance by both of us had finally triumphed. I watched her try a few more times, each success making her a little braver. When she'd had enough, I lifted her to a flat rock and dried her off with the towel, and once she was dressed again, we shoved off, leaving the site clean and tidy for the bear that was probably sleeping off its pork and beans.

We kept to the south side of the lake. The wind was strong as we crossed the wide mouth of the arm, but once near the shore on the other side, it was easy paddling. My confidence in travelling with Suzanne had risen considerably since our first morning on Canoe Lake. There had been a period of adjustment, and it was I who had to do the adjusting.

We cruised along the shoreline, which here ran to the southwest. This brought the wind against our right side, but its push was easily countered by paddling on the left. I stayed just deep enough to keep the paddle from hitting the rocky bottom that I could see sliding beneath us. The next stop on our itinerary was Tom Thomson Lake, which would lead us back to Canoe Lake via a route slightly different from the one we'd come in on. The only portage of any length was the 1,400 into Littledoe, and this was OK as it would bring us closer to our starting point. After that, the only one left was the 250 from Joe Lake into Canoe Lake, then straight to the beach at the Portage Store.

Suzanne's skinny shoulders worked up and down as her arms went back and forth with the paddle. It was a big piece of wood for such a little person, and after a few minutes she gave up and sat nibbling on one of her cookies. I hadn't heard a single word of complaint from her about anything, and any camp chore I asked her to do she did willingly. Having my undivided attention every day was a novelty in itself, and the two of us were just happy being in each other's company in the embrace of the park.

Now into day four of our trip, I had come a long way from the apprehension I felt for her safety on day one, when we'd pushed off into the wind at Canoe Lake. The undercurrent of worry remained, that a fainting spell or seizure could recur at any moment, but her enthusiasm for our adventure made the possibility seem remote. Neither my wife, Bev, nor I knew of any incidence of this sort of thing in our families, and we wondered if the problems associated with her pregnancy might have had something to do with it. The fainting spells and seizures appeared to be triggered by pain. The first one happened when she was about six months old. She bumped her head while being given a sponge bath in the kitchen sink. Instead of crying, she went limp like a rag doll, and the colour drained from her face. It was ten seconds of panic before she regained consciousness. At the time, the possibility that epilepsy might be the cause never entered our minds as she had not exhibited the classic symptoms. Months went by and she was walking before it happened again, when she was playing with another child and they bumped heads. She came straight over to me, her eyes glassy, and as I picked her up she sagged in my arms. Then later there were two grand mal seizures. Both times Bev was alone with her and could scarcely hold her because of the convulsions.

Considering how debilitating epilepsy can be, she was fortunate that it seemed to have been brought under control by a couple of pills, and as she grew older it disappeared from her life altogether.

On the way across the mouth of the arm, I kept an eye out for the red Chestnut but saw neither it nor Lloyd at his fishing perch. A cedarstrip-and-canvas model was the first canoe I had ever set foot in, though I doubt it was a Chestnut. I was eighteen and had taken a summer job as a counsellor at Camp Boulderwood, the children's camp on Gull Lake in Muskoka's cottage country north of Toronto, and since one of my duties would be to take the kids canoeing, I had to learn in a hurry how to use one. On my first lesson, fully clothed and practising the draw stroke in a manner I thought would look like I knew what I was doing, I capsized a paddle-length from the dock, to everyone's amusement. The canoes were forest green, and I still remember our waterfront director having wide orange bands painted on the bottoms so they could be more easily spotted if they overturned out on the lake. Whether this was before or after my mishap, I can't recall. The canoes took a beating from the camp's residents, boys and girls from about the ages of eight to fifteen, but they served faithfully and provided many summers of fun. It wouldn't surprise me if some of them were still in service. It would be a grand day if I came across one for sale that could be traced back to Boulderwood. I'd buy it on the spot.

We drifted past a couple of campsites and rounded the point from which we could now see the west end of the lake. I stuck to our route along the shore's circuitous margin, crossing open water only at the mouth of a small bay that would have taken us east again. Some crows, diving and wheeling around one another, passed us and descended into a tall spruce, where they hopped among the branches in a chorus of guttural cawing as though caught up in a heated debate. My memory flashed back to a peculiar incident involving crows that had happened to me years ago on this very lake. I made a mental note to tell Suzanne about it once we had set up our next camp.

We bumped ashore and went up the embankment to the Minnesing chimneys. A well-worn footpath connected one chimney to the next, a sure sign they were a curiosity to passing canoeists. They were made of fieldstone and mortar, with brick inserts for the hearth, and appeared to be about twenty-five feet high. A metal pipe projecting from the mortar ran horizontally across each hearth, perhaps for heating water. The mantles, hewn from large blocks of stone, were perfectly level.

"Is this where those people stayed?"

"It's where the lady who gave you the cookies stayed with her parents and sisters a long, long time ago."

"What's that?"

I looked to where Suzanne was pointing. Partly hidden in the bushes was the rusted skeleton of a bunk bed, listing but still standing. Pieces of bent pipe lay scattered about. Three wide stone steps in the midst of the trees going nowhere and remnants of the building's wooden framework and a wood-fired cast-iron kitchen stove. I wished Grace were here to walk us through the place and breathe her life into it.

When I first paddled past Minnesing in the early 1960s, the chimneys were a prominent feature, sticking up out of the surrounding trees. Back then, I knew nothing of the history of the place or how it had met its fate. Today, even the chimneys have disappeared, due either to thickening forest cover or collapse. While the location of the site is marked on the map, I suspect most paddlers pass by without a thought as to what stood there once upon a time. But the Minnesing name lives on with the Minnesing Mountain Bike Trail, located southeast of the former lodge, just off Highway 60. It is described as steep, hilly, rugged, muddy and strewn with roots and rocks, unsuitable for small children and out-of-shape adults. In other words, what canoe trippers call a portage.

We poked around, looking for a small artifact we might keep as a souvenir.

"Do you see anything?" I said.

Suzanne shook her head, then took a few steps, and bending down, picked up a small mauve-coloured bottle.

"There's writing on it," she said, handing it to me.

It was rectangular in shape, two inches wide, and counting the extended neck, about six inches long. The embossed lettering read Dr. Chase's Syrup, Linseed and Turpentine, Edmanson Bates and Co., with the number 149 on the bottom.

"I wonder what was in that," I said. "It looks like a medicine bottle." Cough syrup? The thought of swallowing linseed extract and turpentine was worse than the cod liver oil I'd had to endure when a child. Decades later, I would think to look up Dr. Chase on the internet. There I found a photograph of the same mauve bottle, advertised as an antique. It was for sale for twenty-two dollars. The syrup it once contained was extolled for healing and soothing the bronchial tubes and lungs.

With our prize in hand, we went back to the canoe. Suzanne put it in her pack and took out her last cookie, while I spread the map out on the ground.

"This is where we are," I said, pointing to the Minnesing site, "and this is where we'll go today." I indicated Tom Thomson Lake. "We'll camp there for two nights and then we'll go to Nana's."

"Where's the car?" she said.

"It's at the parking lot. Can you find it? I showed it to you the other day."

She looked at the map, and I could see her eyes wandering all over the place.

"It's right here," I said. "And there's Littledoe Lake next to Tom Thomson Lake and here's where we are right now. The only thing is, see this red line, we have to walk from here on Burnt Island all the way over to Littledoe Lake. It's a pretty long walk. We'll have to do it three times to carry all our stuff."

I showed her the red line between Burnt Island and the Otterslides, which she had hiked yesterday, to try giving her an idea of our next portage's length. The Littledoe portage was five hundred yards longer, but on the map, I could scarcely see the difference myself. Two hours would put us on Littledoe, and from there it was an easy paddle through the connecting link to Tom Thomson Lake. The total area of the two lakes would fit into the west half of Burnt Island Lake. They had nearly twenty-five campsites altogether, a good indicator of their accessibility.

"Finish your cookie and we'll get going." I said. The cottonball clouds had begun to link up into bigger grey-tinted ones. We'd been lucky with the weather, but if rain was in the forecast, I wanted to have the tent pitched ahead of it.

The portage from Burnt Island to Littledoe also connected along the way with the landing at Baby Joe Lake where we'd met Merv and his family. This puts it in a perfect location for weekend trips: from Canoe Lake to Littledoe on Saturday, and then down through the Joes and back to Canoe on Sunday. It also means that unless you like company in the bush, and lots of it, forget about this route on a long weekend.

I took the canoe through first. Like many trippers, and like those voyageurs carrying their 180-pound loads over a portage, I have a particular rate of travel with a canoe on my head, a certain rhythm that I slip into, like paddling, especially if the portage is more or less level and short on rocks and tree roots. And once up and moving, it's a rhythm you don't like disturbed, especially after the first two or three hundred yards when your comfort zone is beginning to evaporate under the weight. Age and travelling with friends who viewed canoe trips as a holiday and not an endurance test would slow me down, but generally I functioned best at a kind of slow dogtrot. It was probably imagination, but because the dogtrot made the portage end sooner, it seemed easier than walking. To quote Bill Mason again, "Portaging is like hitting yourself on the head with a hammer: it feels good when you stop."

In truth, it is reported that Mason actually enjoyed portaging in a perverse sort of way. Yes, it's strenuous, especially when it's long or up and down hills or a mix of the two, but the reasoning goes that when you have to work that hard to reach a particular lake that all day you've been envisaging camping beside, your appreciation of the goal achieved is magnified tenfold when compared with arriving there by car. On a trip with two other adults and six teenagers through the Barron River system in 1996, we crossed Ooze Lake (well named) in sultry heat and took a break in the vicinity of what is shown on the map as The Cascades. While most of us cooled off in the river, one of our party went exploring, and on returning, casually mentioned that she had walked past a parking lot. Between the paddle and the air-conditioned chariot, who had the richer experience? To this day, mention of Ooze Lake and its leech-infested portage landing is a bond among the nine of us.

Like the other portages on this trip, this one would be at a walk. In order to keep my eye on Suzanne, she would have to lead the way, and she had no reason to be in a hurry. I plodded along behind her and at one hundred yards called her back on track when she veered off toward Baby Joe's beach. She paused for just a moment to look at the sand and water, then turned and carried on down the trail, her red pack strapped to her shoulders, its only cargo the punctured butterscotch pudding tin I'd kept as a souvenir, the medicine bottle, some of the rocks she'd collected and the faint smell of tuna. Barbie and her wardrobe were in my clothes pack, as Suzanne likely would want her in the tent to play with if we were kept undercover by rain. I had explained that the smell of our lunch from the day before might attract animals and that it would be better to leave her stuff out of it for the time being. The bear had sneaked back during the night, I told her, and found the cans in the water. It had made the holes to get the pudding. She was puzzled about how it had known which can to pick for the pudding, and a little upset, I thought, that it had gotten something she'd been planning to eat herself.

This was our fourth day. Two more to go. I wondered if Suzanne might be getting homesick by now. She seemed perfectly content with her nomadic life in the woods, no doubt our good luck with the weather playing its part. Rain, wet clothes and damp bedding would have changed the tenor of our holiday. You have to expect that sort of thing, but if you can get away without it, so much the better. We passed a party of two canoes hiking the other way, and when we were clear of them, I called for a rest stop.

I set the canoe down beside the trail and untied my life jacket. I hadn't worked up much of a sweat. Our progress was slow anyway, so I might just as well take it easy.

"How far is it to Little Lake?"

"Not too far. It's Littledoe Lake."

"Does it have a beach like the other lake?"

"I don't remember. We'll see when we get there."

I lay down with my hands under my head.

"Somebody cut that tree," she said.

A park warden's chainsaw had done its work on the trunk of a huge birch that had recently fallen over and blocked the trail. The sawdust looked fresh. I got up, and standing one of the sawn pieces on end, brushed it clean.

"Let's see if we can find out how old the tree is," I said.

I showed her the growth rings and how to tell what years the tree grew more than other years and how that would tell us something about past weather patterns in the park. We tallied up nearly seventy rings before the tree's rotted core obliterated further evidence of its age.

"When this tree started to grow," I said, "there were no cars or airplanes or TVs. It's pretty old."

"Do all the trees have rings?"

"Yes. All the trees have rings. Let's peel off some of the loose bark from these cut pieces and put them in your pack. We can use it for a fire starter tonight."

I helped her with a couple of strips, then let her do it, as she seemed to be having fun peeling it back. I lay down again, looking up into the leafy canopy. In the sun, the leaves of the maple were lime green, the ones higher up casting their dancing shadows over the ones below. I looked at my watch. Early afternoon yet. In a couple of hours we would be pitching our camp for the last time. I wondered how long it seemed to Suzanne that she had been out here. In a few days she had done a lot. She came over to show me the handful of birch strips she'd peeled off, then put them in her pack and pulled out the tin.

"How did the bear bite through it?" she said. She put a finger in one of the holes.

"It's made of aluminum. It's a very soft metal. You could bite a hole in it if you wanted to."

She crinkled her nose and put the tin back in the pack. One day in the distant future I would give it to her. What images, I wondered, would she see when she held it in her hand?

"I guess we'd better get going," I said. "We still have to do this walk two more times."

We rested twice more, the second time unknowingly within a short distance of the lake. It was a roller-coaster kind of trail with ups and downs and twists and turns. The last time I had been over it was before Suzanne was born. I set the canoe down at the side of the trail close to the water and pulled off my life jacket. A breeze was coming in off the lake, and I stood with my hands on my hips, letting it blow through my damp T-shirt. Anyone who has sweated a long portage on a hot day can tell you how good this feels.

There were a couple of canoes on the lake, two passengers in each but no gear. They had downed paddles, and with arms and legs draped over the gunnels, were sunning themselves. It was a lazy and pleasurable way to spend a summer afternoon, rocking gently, eyes half-closed, fingers trailing in the water's cooling silky smoothness. You were like a baby in a cradle with nothing but the splash of a fish or whir of a dragonfly to disturb your dreaming.

I took Suzanne's hand and we started back for the second load. I enjoy the return trip over a portage. There is nothing to carry. You can relax and take in the scenery you missed while going the other way under load. Following a forest trail as it winds toward a distant lake is part of the wilderness experience. The western side of the park with its abundant hardwoods is particularly pretty, especially in the autumn when the maples and oaks are a blaze of red and orange and yellow. The park is quieter then too, getting ready to bed down for another winter. It is a nice time to plan a visit. Mosquitos are scarce. There are numerous hiking trails easily accessible from the highway that make for a good day's family outing.

We padded along, just the two of us in the woods, our footfalls soft on the packed earth. "I never found the companion that was so companionable as solitude," Thoreau wrote. I wonder, had he been a father, would he have made allowance in that solitude for children. My trip with Suzanne remains one of the richer experiences of my life. Considering how easy it could have been for it never to have happened, I was lucky, and while in hindsight I wouldn't have risked it again, I'm grateful for it.

The portage curved to the right and went up a grade. At the top, a pole had been nailed between two tree trunks for a canoe rest at a height of about eight feet. Without putting the canoe down, you could place the forward end on the pole and take the weight off your shoulders. These rests are welcome respites, but hard to spot when you have a canoe on your head. Unless someone walking in front is keeping watch, you're just as likely to go right past one without seeing it. I hadn't noticed this one on the way to Littledoe.

A sudden beating of wings erupted in the bushes beside us. We both jumped.

"What's that?" Suzanne said, grabbing my arm.

A grouse, keeping low to the ground, shot away in a whir among the trees, too fast for Suzanne to catch sight of it. These birds seem to have a penchant for waiting until the last second before fleeing and they never fail to give your heart a jolt. They are common to Algonquin, but through the years, about the only place I've encountered them is on a portage and not all that often. It was a ruffed grouse, I told Suzanne, and I described how they thump their wings to stake out their territory and attract females. In his field guide, Peterson waxed poetic about the bird: "At a distance the muffled thumping is so hollow that sometimes it hardly registers as an exterior sound, but seems rather a disturbing series of vibrations within the ear itself."

We passed the sawn birch and in a few minutes reached Baby Joe and walked down to the water. The sky was close to overcast now. It looked like we were finally going to get some rain.

A canoe had cut a groove in the border of damp sand that traced the waterline. Beside it there were two sets of footprints, large prints and slightly smaller ones, and the braided imprint of a piece of rope that someone had stepped on. The footprints came and went, but the ones leading landward looked slightly deeper, as they would be if unloading gear. And odds were that the rope was tied to the bow, a further indication the canoe had come ashore. The evidence looked fresh, and I said that if we hurried up to the Burnt Island landing just two hundred yards ahead, we might find the canoe still there and we could check if I was right. We should see two people, likely a man and a woman, with a canoe that had a keel and a rope tied to the bow. It had to have gone toward Burnt Island since we hadn't passed anybody on our way back from Littledoe. Suzanne responded to my detective reasoning by asking if she could go swimming first. My forensics hadn't made much of an impression. I coaxed her to carry on with the promise of a swim when we got to our campsite, which I said I wanted to reach so I could get the tent up in case of rain.

As we broke out from the woods onto the Burnt Island landing, I counted six canoes surrounded by a jumble of gear that I had to pick my way through to get to our own stuff. I noted that three or four canoes had ropes tied to their bows. Adults and children milled noisily about, and unseen back in the trees, someone was yelling "Molson! Molson! Here Molson!" followed by a piercing whistle. I hadn't a clue who was coming and who was going.

10

*Education is the most powerful weapon
you can use to change the world.*
– Nelson Mandela

As we broke from the channel connecting Littledoe to Tom Thomson, I got out the binoculars. The site on our right and another on the point ahead were occupied, but by a stroke of luck, it appeared no one had claimed the site on the small island a short distance off to our left. I could feel the spring in the paddle as I muscled down on it and made a beeline for our night's bivouac.

I had been through Tom Thomson before but had never camped on its shore. It was too close to the highway, just a half-day paddle, to be considered for a stopover. I always pressed on through to the 2,300-yard portage out of the north end of Thomson into minuscule Ink Lake and thence by creek to McIntosh Lake. From there it was an easy go the next day via meandering McIntosh Creek to Big Trout.

The island was elongated in shape and almost indistinguishable against the surrounding mainland. An inviting landing highlighted the campsite at its north end with a tiny meadow of green grass. As we came ashore, I noted that it looked to be popular. Someone had made a log-frame table with a plywood top. There was a clothesline with clothespins made of split sticks. Three heavy logs, their upsides made flat with an axe for more comfortable sitting, formed a triangle around the firepit. And back in the trees was an amenity to which I had no objection — an outhouse, complete with a door on rusty hinges, a roll of toilet paper and an Archie and Jughead paperback.

In a few minutes we had the tent up and the sleeping bags and the rain gear stowed inside. I debated about having an early supper. It was nearing four thirty, still a bit early, but if we waited till later we might be eating our meal in the rain, or not eating at all if it was really coming down.

"Are you hungry?" I said.

Our lunch had been a light snack of cheese and a raisin-peanut mix while on the move.

"What are we having?"

"Pizza and root beer."

She looked at me, her nose crinkling up.

"No we're not."

"We can have it on the way to Nana's at a restaurant. How about that?"

She responded with a big grin.

"Do you want to eat now or later?"

"Now. Can I go swimming first?"

I looked at the dull grey sky that had closed in on Thomson, darkening the lake's surface.

"OK, but just a short one. I'll watch."

I pulled out my pipe and tamped a thumbnail of Amphora into the bowl. The man, after whom this lake was named, canoed these parts in the early years of the twentieth century, capturing the lakes, trees, rocks and sky in paintings that would give Algonquin Park to the world and immortality to the artist. Canvases with titles like *Jack Pine*, *Summer Day*, *April in Algonquin Park* and *The West Wind* are the legacy of Tom Thomson, whose death continues to be something of a mystery. An article in the *Toronto Star* some years ago stated that "there persists in its [Algonquin Park's] wild heartland one of the most romantic mysteries in Canada's history. It is the dramatic saga of the untimely death — some say murder — of acclaimed Canadian artist Tom Thomson, forerunner of the Group of Seven."

Thomson was just shy of his fortieth birthday when he died in 1917. His overturned canoe was found in Canoe Lake on July 8, and eight days later his body surfaced. It was reported that there were signs of a hard blow to his head, but the coroner, who arrived *after* Thomson's burial, concluded his death had been accidental. Thomson's body, it is believed, was subsequently moved by his family from the cemetery at Canoe Lake to the church cemetery in Leith, Ontario, close to the family farm. In 1956, when the original grave was dug up in an effort to find some answers to the ongoing controversy, a body was found but deemed to be someone other than Thomson. Much has been written about all of this, but the definitive conclusion remains elusive. I think Roy MacGregor's book *Northern Light: The Enduring Mystery of Tom Thomson and the Woman Who Loved Him* comes as close as we're going to get to understanding the likely cause of this Canadian icon's tragic death.

A good place to view many of Thomson's paintings is the remarkable McMichael gallery in Kleinburg, Ontario. The old, weather-beaten shack he used as his studio during the winter months is there too, having been moved from its original downtown Toronto site to Kleinburg in 1962.

Camping on an island appeals to most people, a fact easily verified when you go looking for firewood. Although there are usually some deadfalls, the supply of fuel is often pretty lean on a small island. This one, however, seemed to have enough. We wouldn't have to scout along the mainland shore for a load. Suzanne, still in her bathing suit with a towel draped over her shoulders, helped me gather what was needed to cook our supper and enjoy an evening campfire, weather permitting.

As we sat eating our meal, the strong tremolo of a loon broke the quiet. A second one answered, and after a few minutes we saw the pair a little way out on the lake. They kept dipping their heads into the water looking for fish. I couldn't see any chicks hitching a ride on their backs, as they sometimes do.

Had Thomson ever landed on this island, sat on this very shore where we sat watching the loons diving for their dinner? Considering the many summers he spent in the park, there was no reason to believe it wasn't a possibility. One of his paintings might have originated from here. While his career as an artist was cut short, his impact on Canadian art and Canadian identity is inestimable. We'll never know what might have been had he been granted a longer life.

Tiny water rings sprouted on the lake. I held out the back of my hand to the sky. It seemed our luck had run out. It felt more like a mist than rain, but it could be the harbinger of heavier weather to come.

"Hurry and finish eating," I said, "then go into the tent and get dressed."

I made a quick check of the site and then ran the pack up the tree I had already selected. We were as ready as could be for whatever the weather had in store. Rain slow to move in could be slow to move out, so we were probably in for a night of it. I was glad the plan was to stay put tomorrow. Packing up wet camping gear is never fun. The only time you don't care is when your next stop is the parking lot, where it all gets tossed into the trunk of your car for the drive home.

Suzanne had put on a sweater and pants. We pulled on our raincoats and stood with our hands in the rubber pockets, staring at the lake. The loons had moved off to the south end of the island, calling back and forth every now and then.

"Remember those noisy crows we saw today near the chimneys?" I said.

She nodded inside her rain hood, not looking up from the water, as though mesmerized by the rings and the tiny bubbles the raindrops created, appearing and vanishing in front of her.

"I have a story about some crows I saw up here before you were born. Do you want to hear it?"

She nodded again. I wasn't sure if it would interest her or not. But it had a strangeness about it that I thought might catch her attention.

I was on a trip with a friend a decade earlier, and we were camped at a site not far from where Suzanne and I had the visit from our first bear. It was light but still very early in the morning. I was lying in my sleeping bag only half-awake, not wanting to get up, when I heard what sounded like the voices of little children. Between the snores of my friend, I strained to hear. They were faint sounds, as though coming from a considerable distance, and at first I thought a family was canoeing past. But the minutes ticked by and the voices remained — faint, high pitched and unintelligible. While the voices sounded childlike, I got the impression a serious but restrained conversation was going on, highlighted by intervals of silence. I unzipped the tent slowly and stuck my head out.

The lake lay anvil-flat with a thick shroud of mist blanketing its surface. Canoeists just offshore would pass unseen. I cocked an ear, trying to pinpoint the sounds. The morning was very still, the pale mist making the stillness even deeper. Pulling on my runners, I crawled outside. Dew beaded the roof of the tent and the groundsheet spread over the stacked firewood. I took a few steps, stopped, listened. The voices were garbled, like a foreign language I couldn't quite identify. But they weren't coming off the water. I turned and looked into the forest that crowded around our campsite. The talkers were somewhere back there, hidden among the dark trees and underbrush. I went around the tent and stepped into the trees. They were off to the right. Carefully, I moved in that direction, pressing aside wet branches and peering ahead expectantly, hoping my approach would not be detected. Each time the voices fell silent, I waited the few seconds until they picked up again, using the conversation itself as a cover for any sounds I might make.

Ahead through the trees, I could see a lighter patch of ground, a clearing barely illuminated by the mist-shrouded sun. I bent low and crept toward the clearing's perimeter, taking advantage of every bit of cover to get as close as I could to the voices. And then suddenly, there they were, standing in a circle, five crows in blue-black dress, talking to each other in their curious croaking voices. The scene was primordial. I had stumbled onto something heretofore unknown to mankind, or so it was easy to imagine at that moment — a secret society of crows meeting at dawn in a forest clearing! They faced toward the centre, sometimes taking turns to speak, sometimes all chiming in together. But it was low-key, almost polite, not the melee of wheeling and cawing birds that Suzanne and I had seen near the chimneys. And then as one, they fell silent, as if to some hidden signal, listening, perhaps, for warning signs of danger, and when assured of safety, carrying on again with their confabulation. They were evenly spaced in their strange assembly, and except for a step this way and that, kept their places.

It was an oddly fascinating spectacle, men in feathers singing and dancing in a circle as the sun rose to drive away the darkness — such a transformation was easy to envision. The roots of man lie deep within the natural world. They are the brick-and-mortar foundation of our existence, and we are bound to them in ways we have forgotten. We need to make the effort to find and understand them once again if we are to point the way toward a healthy future for the planet and ourselves. In his book *The Human Relationship with Nature*, Peter Kahn references the finding of more than a hundred studies confirming that the corollary of time spent with nature includes stress reduction. This, to my mind, is self-evident. It is something we feel intuitively, something that lets us exhale, lets the shoulder and neck muscles relax and fills our senses with the smells and sounds of the outdoors. Children are not exempt from stress, especially in the twenty-first century. Giving them the chance to experience nature's embrace at an early age is a constructive ingredient in the development of the person they will become. In these days of virtual reality, we must not lose sight of the importance of primary experience. Children explore the world through their senses, and one of the best realms for that exploration is nature.

"What were the crows talking about?" Suzanne asked when

I finished.

"I don't know. Crows are pretty smart birds. Maybe they have a language of their own, just like us."

The rain had picked up a little, whispering on the lake and dripping from the hoods of our raincoats. It was the kind of innocuous weather that could sneak up on you when paddling across a lake and grab you with a chill. Shaking ourselves like a couple of dogs, we crawled into the tent. The rain drummed on the canvas, reducing our four-by-six-foot space to a world of dim light and muffled sound. I stuffed the raincoats into the tent corners at our feet and stretched out on my sleeping bag, enjoying the excuse of rain for not having to think of something for us to do. Suzanne sat cross-legged and got her Barbie into pink pyjamas with marabou around the collar and cuffs. Barbie seemed to have an inexhaustible wardrobe.

"Did Mummy make those?" I said.

"Yep."

Most of the outfits had been sewn by her mother, who liked working with the patterns and colours on a miniature scale. Hopefully the costumes would keep her amused until she got sleepy. We still had another couple of hours before dusk, and a small child cooped up in a small space for a long period is not a good recipe. But we weren't going anywhere, so we would have to make the best of it.

In the woods, I usually sleep better when it rains. Nocturnal sounds are obscured by the rain's patter on the tent, and it will lull you into dreamland more quickly than a dull book. It shuts down that primitive part of the brain that says stay alert or be eaten. Things that go bump in the night can't be heard, so you just relax.

I read a few pages of my book, and for twenty minutes we played needle and thread, the name Suzanne had given to a word game I'd dreamed up the previous summer. One person would give two words, such as *needle* and *thread*, and the other person would have to come up with a complementary third word, such as *sew*. We worked on a camping theme until we started repeating ourselves. She stumped me with *red* and *sharp* for the red-eyed, sharp-beaked loon, and I was impressed that she had remembered this observation despite her distress at the time.

The low rumble of rolling thunder, still far away, was a portent of what could come our way. The pitter-patter cadence of the rain picked up.

"Who are you going to invite to your birthday party?"

She named a few of her friends. In three months she would turn six years old. She had checked off the red bicycle she wanted in the Eaton's catalogue, and an array of Barbie doll accessories she figured she needed.

"Can you ride a two-wheeler?"

"Yep. You can show me."

She had a little two-wheeler with training wheels, which I removed and then replaced when she fell and skinned her knee. I didn't want her falling and bumping her head. We would get her the red bicycle and a helmet to go with it.

We tried a few rounds of Xs and Os on the back page of my notebook, then sat turning the pages of the outhouse paperback that I had tossed into the tent when it looked like we were going to have to take cover early. We read about the shenanigans of Archie, Jughead, Veronica and Betty, and Suzanne laughed when I told her that as a little boy, I had worn a cap something like Jughead's, a cream-coloured beanie with a zigzag rim and pop bottle caps attached by taking the cork liner out of a cap, pressing the cap against the beanie and then jamming the cork back in from the other side. She hooked her arm through mine and leaned against my chest, and after a while, as I droned on, she fell asleep. When I was sure she was out for the count, I got her into her sleeping bag and snuggled down into mine. It wasn't dark yet, but happily there was nothing else to do. The rain beat a steady tattoo against the canvas. We slept like logs.

As often happens in Algonquin Park after a night of rain, the morning dawned with blue sky and bright sunshine. The ground was wet and the trees still dripped, but there was not a cloud to be seen. Protected by the canoe and groundsheet, the firewood was tinder dry, and with a few strips of birchbark from Suzanne's pack, I had a crackling fire and boiling water in no time. I lowered the canoe pack, made myself a cup of coffee, and sat by the fire's warmth, looking out at the lake. If there had been a bear in camp during the night, it had passed unnoted.

A canoe floated on the flat, blue water near the entrance to the channel leading back to Littledoe, its two passengers with fishing rods over the side. At the campsite on the north shore directly across from us, smoke mixed with early sunlight hung lazily in the trees. Someone came down to the shore and stood with hands in pockets, soaking up the warmth of the sun after the wet night. I had woken only once, briefly, to a drumming of rain and the distant mournful wail of a loon rising out of the dark and then trailing off. As usual, Suzanne had slept straight through and was still asleep. This morning, since we weren't moving on, I would let her rouse herself.

I ran through the list of fun things we could do for our last day.

Explore Thomson, collect driftwood sculptures, hike the portage to Ink Lake and go for a swim, maybe back at the Baby Joe beach. All we would have to carry were our towels and bathing suits. If I was really energetic, I could carry the canoe over to McIntosh. There was a dilapidated and abandoned cabin on the shore, with a beat-up old bed in it, or there was the last time I was through there a few years before. It might have been a ranger post once, or a nineteenth-century homestead or a bunkhouse from logging days. I remembered the campers who had set up next to it for the night, a flotilla of canoes from a boys' camp, maybe Algonquin's Camp Ahmek. It was around suppertime and they were eating corned beef and jam sandwiches. We stopped to talk to one of the counsellors and were invited ashore to have a sandwich too, which we did. As I say, every meal in the bush is delicious.

    I rummaged around for the string hammock I'd brought and hadn't bothered to use thus far, and strung it between two trees near the water. Washed clean by the rain and in the white light of the morning sun, the day had a vibrancy to it, an intense energy that in the wilderness silence seemed to hum, ready to burst into celebration of its glory. I shoved off with my foot, the hammock's swing shaking down cold raindrops from the canopy of leaves, the air redolent of damp earth and wood smoke. I couldn't agree more with the sentiment expressed by park guide Ralph Bice, who was born in 1900 and received the Order of Canada, one of the country's highest honours, in his old age. I don't remember exactly how it went, but basically, he was saying that anyone who's been to Algonquin Park is going to be disappointed when they get to heaven. It was hard for me to imagine how heaven could be any better than this. God probably spent weekends here.

The park is not everyone's cup of tea, but for me, Bice hit the nail on the head. I laughed the first time I saw the quote on a wall of the McMichael gallery. In a single sentence, he had tapped into the heart of what so many of us who travel here believe. Algonquin is a kind of heaven on earth, and we'll miss it when we're gone.

Suddenly, Suzanne was standing beside me. I hadn't heard her unzip the tent.

"Hi! Did you have a good sleep?" She nodded, looking out at the lake. "Did your sleeping bag stay dry?"

"Yep."

"Ready for breakfast? We can talk about what we're going to do today."

I made her a cup of warm hot chocolate, then used the last of the wood to bring the water to a boil for our porridge. The fire crackled and flared up. Sparks of grey ash floated into the air through light and shade, filtering through the trees into the sky.

We spent the day on Thomson, neither of us with an inclination to do anything that might be strenuous. When I suggested the beach at Baby Joe for a swim, Suzanne replied by saying maybe we could find a swimming place closer. We made a leisurely tour around the shore, noting a web of clotheslines at one campsite that sagged with the weight of its cargo of wet sleeping bags. After a soaker of a night, there is nothing more welcome than a sunny morning. In those cold, soggy hours of darkness and fitful sleep, even the atheist prays for the sun.

At a couple of places where firewood pickings looked good and were easily accessible, we went ashore to gather up two or three armloads, and in a semi-clearing against a low hill, spotted a swath of raspberry bushes ripe with fruit. We fed on the berries just like bears out of hibernation. There were so many, we decided to return later to fill our cookpot. Wild raspberries stirred into the morning's porridge or dropped into pancake batter would add a tasty zing to tomorrow's start.

We went along the west shore to the lake's north end where it pinches to a narrow opening leading to a small bay and the McIntosh portage. As we drifted past the campsites on either side, we heard someone shout and then saw a canoe moving in our direction through the trees. The carrier brought it to the water's edge, and lifting it easily from his shoulders, set it on the ground. Two boys in their early teens followed, then two more canoes and another half-dozen children around the same age as the first two, both boys and girls, all loaded down with packs and paddles and life jackets.

I asked Suzanne if she would like to go to camp by herself when she was older.

"Could Laurie come too?" she said.

"Sure. You could both go. There would probably be swimming every day. And you could go on a canoe trip with a bunch of other kids, like these kids."

We watched as the incoming traffic continued to build like an invasion force, each new arrival of boat or child adding to the growing chaos at the beachhead. Apparently two or three separate groups had converged and were coming through the 2,300-yard portage together. It must have been quite a sight on the other side at tiny Ink Lake and along the creek connecting it to McIntosh. I hung back about a hundred feet, the two of us watching the unfolding scene as though it were a show spilling out of the woods just for us. Each time I thought the last canoe had come through, another arrived until there were maybe a dozen, some of them at the shore, others scattered through the trees just behind, and seemingly untold numbers of children scrambling among them like ants, their backpacks dropped willy-nilly. How they were going to sort everything out would be a challenge. I paddled past slowly, returning the waves of a few, the whole gang of them settling in noisily for a snack. A man standing at the water's edge said good morning.

"Must have been a busy portage," I said.

He laughed. "Thank God our next stop is the parking lot."

I followed the curve of the bay, and in a few minutes we were back on Thomson proper where there was not a person to be seen nor a sound to be heard.

After a cheese-sandwich lunch at the campsite, we got in an hour's swimming, then went back to the berry patch and filled the cookpot a third of the way up with raspberries. They were sweet and tangy and way too good to save until later. We ate them all while sitting in the canoe in the shade of a birch that leaned out over the water. It was cooler here, and with a bit of a breeze it would have been perfect. But the air was still and humid, and out on the lake the sun sucked water out of every pore.

Back at the campsite, I moved the hammock into the deeper shadows of the woods and held it steady while Suzanne, her T-shirt stained with raspberry juice, climbed in with the Archie book. She had liked books from an early age and her reading was improving, but with the pictures on every page, she could invent her own stories as to what the characters were doing. I gave her a push.

The element of imagination is important in a child's development, and I can't help but wonder if it isn't under siege, what with all the high-tech toys we have at our fingertips nowadays. Why try to imagine anything when your electronic world has you believing it is more imaginative than you could ever be anyway? Children need and deserve the opportunity to discover that there is another kind of electricity they can plug into, electricity that will jump-start their own imagination and enrich both their physical and mental health. Places like Algonquin Park give them that chance — where living is stripped to its bare essentials and one's inner resources are tested daily.

I have thought that it would serve mankind well if governments considered outdoor education as an essential ingredient, like reading, writing and arithmetic, in the lives of children, not as an extracurricular activity. Imagine a Department of Nature, or better yet a Department of Wilderness, the latter lending it a spirit of adventure, with a mandate to ensure that over the course of their elementary and high-school years, children truly learn about the balance of the natural world and our pivotal place in it. Symbolically, I suggest that funding for outdoor education should reflect a percentage of the country's defence budget. As I write this, three percent of Canada's defence budget would cover the cost of a couple of fighter jets, about $50 million. Imagine what could be accomplished by earmarking that amount for the health of the planet and the life it supports? It's the only ship we've got. There are no lifeboats if it sinks. The offerings paid worldwide to the god of weaponry are staggering when you think of the good those billions of dollars could do to promote a better world. If every able country chipped in, the payback over time would far outweigh the cost. The level of a child's participation would relate to his or her abilities, and it wouldn't take much in the way of encouragement to get each child happily involved. Children are adventurous, they relish challenges, they like to test themselves when they're in the company of friends and classmates having fun. In the woods, an esprit de corps forms quickly, even among strangers. Learning and playing together in the great outdoors, individuals become a team progressing toward a common goal, in this case a healthy ecosystem. And what naturally evolves from this is a citizenry respectful of Mother Earth. The concept of wilderness, that "geography of hope," will become a bond that is common to everyone everywhere, from generation to generation, an international language that everyone speaks.

Canada is blessed with vast wild spaces that can work wonders on young minds. Its rivers, lakes and forests, its mountains, glaciers and oceans offer children a magical playground of natural wonders. What miracles might we and our children see on this sadly abused planet if we all took the time to really understand that every blow it suffers by our hand is an act of violence against its bounty and the generations to come?

Bruce Chatwin, author of the classic travel book *In Patagonia*, wrote that "our early explorations are the raw materials of our intelligence. Children need paths to explore, to take bearings on the earth in which they live." He compared a child on a journey to a navigator taking bearings in relation to familiar landmarks, and said that if we excavate the memories of childhood, we remember the paths first; things and people second. Some of these paths, we should agree, need to lead through the natural world, through wilderness. We need the great outdoors whether we know it or not. The consumer-oriented aspect of our modern world has shuffled the outdoors to the back of the shelf, but deep down the spiritual ties remain. Speak to the animals, the birds and the earth, the Old Testament commands, and they will teach us. We did this for a hundred thousand years, and measured against this time scale, only recently did we conclude that such communication was no longer required. When Europeans arrived in North America, they found indigenous people who believed in the power and mystery of all living things, people who did communicate with the natural world. Forgetful of their own ancient heritage and enthralled with their technological achievements, these Europeans thought themselves superior to the inhabitants of the lands they overran, and set about to "correct" this divinity of nature with devastating efficiency. But the indigenous peoples, it turns out, had something to tell us, and belatedly have we begun to understand that we are not separate from nature. We are not above and beyond its laws. They form an integral part of our existence and we ignore them at our peril. The prophecy of the Ojibwa people, recognized in an exhibit at Ontario's Petroglyphs Provincial Park, may well be borne out: "There will come a time when other nations will turn to us for the answers, for directions, how to face the uncertain future."

The story of the effects of climate change and environmental pollution in the Arctic is especially telling. You have only to read Sheila Watt-Cloutier's compelling book *The Right to be Cold* to see how devastating these problems can be on an entire society. A Canadian Inuit woman, Watt-Cloutier has spent the better part of her professional career fighting for a healthy environment and for her Arctic people. She went from travelling by dogsled for the first decade of her life to travelling the world in pursuit of the well-being of the planet, work that led to her nomination for the Nobel Peace Prize in 2007. "Leadership," she says, "is about working from a principled and ethical place within yourself." If this belief is due in part to her close ties with nature, and I believe it is, then opening nature's door to our children is an irreplaceable gift.

The legacy of our abuse of the natural world can be traced in part to prominent thinkers from the past. Just as some great writers and philosophers have extolled the value of nature, others have seen it in a less favourable light. The Lord Chancellor of England Francis Bacon, born in 1601, believed that "the ways of nature are to be conquered, not obeyed," and that man "must wrest by force and ingenuity, what little he can for his own use." In the following century, philosopher and physicist Robert Boyle, author of *Empire of Man over the Inferior Creatures of God*, and philosopher John Locke carried the torch Bacon had lit. Boyle argued in favour of understanding the workings of nature in the same way you would understand the workings of a machine, and decried any concept of nature having a benevolent face. If nature is such a good thing for man, he reasoned, "how comes it to pass, that from time to time, she destroys such Multitudes of Men and Beasts, by Earthquakes, Pestilence, Famine and other Anomolus?" As for Locke, he considered land left to nature a waste.

This dominating view of the natural world has been slow to change. We've made some progress in our thinking, but still have a long way to go. There are still those who see only the "waste," but the mindset of men like Boyle and Locke is being challenged. Thanks to the growing number of concerned citizens, our stewardship of the planet is under the microscope. It will take vision, courage and commitment to stop the bleeding and heal the wounds already inflicted. "The clearest way into the universe," said writer, naturalist and environmental philosopher John Muir, "is through a forest wilderness." My take on this is that Muir was talking about our survival. At the age of twenty-five he walked away from his university studies to attend what he called the University of the Wilderness. He travelled the world, and out of those peregrinations grew his belief in conservation of the natural environment. The last time I looked, the internet listed thirty-five books authored by him, all of them reflecting his admiration, love and respect for the benevolence and grandeur of the natural world.

In Frederick Ferré's praise for *The Re-enchantment of the World*, the American philosopher said the book's author, Morris Berman, was "searching for the underpinnings of a new world view that can give rise to a culture capable of relating gently and self-sustainingly to the earth." An educated understanding of the natural world that begins with young children experiencing the outdoors can go a long way to taking us in that direction.

Wilderness means different things to different people. Children don't need the dictionary definition of wilderness, "an uncultivated, uninhabited, or barren region." This is not a description of Algonquin Park, a lushly forested land full of wildlife and happy campers, encompassed on all sides by civilization. For children, it's the perfect introduction. The park interior severs their online connection, which they believe they can't live without, and pushes them into the natural world where physical labour, the elements and camaraderie are their daily companions. Rubbing shoulders with nature will give them the opportunity to see another side of life they might otherwise never know, and maybe they'll be surprised by strengths they never knew they had. Their explorations will enhance the odds of bringing our planet back to health.

"Push me again."

I gave the hammock another push and drew a long, peeled branch from the pile of firewood we had collected, breaking it off about three feet long.

"You can use this to push yourself. When you slow down just stick it in the ground and push to get going again."

I wondered how things were going back home. We had been away five full days without communication. There was always that bit of concern at the back of my mind that if something happened and I was needed, there was simply no way of knowing until I came out of the bush. It could be tougher for those at home imagining the disasters that could befall you on the trail. But what with the rapid advance of technology nowadays, it may not be long before phoning home from your canoe or campsite back in the bush might just be possible. Call me old-fashioned, but the day I figure I need a phone on a canoe trip is the day I hang up my paddle. Self-reliance, one of the highs of wilderness travel, will have lost a round; if things get tough, call home.

I busied myself breaking firewood into convenient lengths, snapping the small stuff over my knee and using a hand and foot for the thicker pieces. Suzanne lay swinging, the stick balanced across her stomach and her head arched back, looking for the red squirrel chattering noisily somewhere above her. How did squirrels get to these islands in the first place? I couldn't imagine them swimming over, and it made no sense for them to leave the safety of the mainland in winter to run across the ice. Maybe we were on a tiny Galapagos where this family of red squirrels had lived for millennia, different from their brethren on the mainland. The things you think of when you have nothing to do.

A spruce cone hit the ground with a thump, then another and another. The red was cutting them loose from the upper branches and would collect them later for the seeds they contained. Suzanne got out of the hammock and picked one up. It oozed a sticky resin.

"How would you like to eat that for your dinner?"

She crinkled her nose and dropped it, her finger stuck to her thumb.

"You'll need hot water to wash that off. Fix the wood for the fire, and I'll put some water on to boil. Then I'll see what's for supper. Use a piece of birchbark from your pack to make a floor, then build a log cabin over it. It'll make a good fire."

I emptied everything out onto the groundsheet, then turned the pack inside out and gave it a shake. From the looks of it, we could stay another couple of days if we wanted, just laze around on the island and eat. I had gone a little overboard with supplies this trip, but there being only one portage of any consequence, it hadn't really been a problem other than getting it all up a tree every night and keeping the frying pan between the contents and the bear's handiwork.

Suzanne bent over the firepit, carefully placing one stick at a time in log cabin formation over some birchbark. We had enough firewood for supper and breakfast and a campfire this evening. And waiting for us, just beyond the clean horizon, were the reds and pinks of a sunset that would melt to green and navy blue and cast the night sky in its veil of stars. Enjoying it beside a crackling fire would be a nice way to finish up the last day of our trip.

11

Algonquin ... a place where people go in order to feel spiritually whole again.

– Joanne Kates

By eight o'clock on this last morning, we were paddling into the sun to Littledoe, then straight south for Joe Lake and the dam where we had eaten our lunch on day one. Our ETA at Canoe Lake beach, about six miles away, was somewhere between noon and one o'clock, just in time for lunch at the restaurant. Suzanne had already made up her mind, the pizza and root beer having been pushed aside for a chocolate milkshake and a cheeseburger.

As we left Littledoe behind, the thickly treed shoreline pressed in from either side, blackening the water with its reflections of spruce and pine and maple, their boughs sweeping out over the dark surface of our homebound path. It looked like an easy run. There was only a light breeze, and the sun hadn't been up long enough to heat the air and coax the deer flies out of the woods to where they could easily find and feast on us in this narrowing channel. They are especially fond of wet feet. Their bite is sudden and painful. Flailing at them with your hands or paddle can be a dicey manoeuvre in a tippy canoe.

We passed a number of campsites, all of them occupied. At one, we were greeted loudly by a wet tail-wagging Irish setter that kept pawing the water as though inviting us to come ashore and play. The air resounded with squeals of children playing some uproarious game in a large blue and orange tent back among the trees. Nearby, a man squatted in front of the firepit, his hair dishevelled, fanning the firepit with a pot lid. I could see neither smoke nor flame. He waved the lid at us as we drifted by.

Accompanied by our water-mirrored images, I paddled a relaxed pace. Day six, a beautiful day of water, sky, trees and light — dazzling, humming light that would have made Van Gogh delirious with its brilliance. Thomson painted in this light, and I have been lucky enough to have paddled through many of the scenes he painted. His *Summer Day* comes immediately to mind, for I have seen that sky a hundred times up here.

Suzanne had taken each day of the trip in stride as though she had done it all before. I wondered what impressions of Algonquin would stand out for her at so young an age. Certainly the swimming, and perhaps the bear stealing her dessert. In his book *Wolf Willow*, Wallace Stegner said he believed that children "exposed to a particular environment at a susceptible age" would perceive in the shapes of that environment all their lives. From his own boyhood experience on a homestead in Eastend, Saskatchewan, during the years of the First World War, he wondered why it was that a "dead loop" in the Whitemud River, known to him for only a few years, should be "so charged with potency" in his unconscious that it constantly recurred in his dreams and in the images he brought up off the typewriter and onto the page. "They lie in me like underground water," he said, "every well I put down taps them."

We all have incidents like this, a memory locked away until some telltale trigger pushes it into consciousness. When I was Suzanne's age, I went with my father, one summer's day, in a yellow tank truck to the fuel depot at the air force station where we lived. The depot stood off by itself near some woods and a raspberry patch. While Dad filled the tanker with aviation fuel, I helped myself to the red-ripe bonanza. To this day, the smell and taste of fresh raspberries remind me, like clockwork, of that pleasant scene. Algonquin would leave something to Suzanne, and in due course it would be revealed. A scene, a particular sound, the whiff of wood smoke on the early morning air, and she will remember.

Children are like sponges, and if we give them good things to soak up when they are very young, these things will in time form the bedrock of the road they build in life. It will take some longer than others to find their way, but the bedrock, that essential foundation, will be there for them. An understanding of and respect for nature needs to be a part of that foundation. "We did not weave the web of life," said North American native leader Chief Seattle. "We are merely a strand in it. Whatever we do to the web we do to ourselves."

In the mid-1990s, I came across a *Toronto Star* report under the banner headline SCIENTISTS FEAR FOR 'HEALTH OF OUR PLANET.' It was covering meetings of the American Association for the Advancement of Science where "in an unprecedented statement... the scientists conceded they are not fully prepared to tackle what they call a growing 'threat to the Earth's life support systems.'" The report then quoted the association's president by saying "science has provided 'tremendous insights into our bodies, our minds, our world, our galaxy and our universe,' but [she] added it has failed to address what she called the greatest challenge of all — 'the future health of our planet.'" The report also indicated that "leading experts say the world's scientific community, governments and the public must act quickly to avoid an impending economic and environmental crisis." This report could have been written today. Contrary to the disbelievers, the threat remains and continues to grow.

Key words in the report include *the public*. Scientists and governments won't solve the problem without help from the rest of us. We have to care and we have to pitch in to work toward that culture capable of relating gently and self-sustainingly to the earth. In his article "The Eleventh Commandment: Toward an Ethic of Ecology," environmental activist Vincent Rossi wrote, "What is needed is for men and women to feel *religious* about nature." And in her book *Exploring Algonquin Park*, Camp Arowhon's director Joanne Kates wrote that "Algonquin Park is a twentieth-century cathedral for the soul, a place where people go in order to feel spiritually whole again." It is no less so in the twenty-first century and will be in the centuries to follow. Our wilderness places are treasures we need to hold close to our hearts.

We broke into pint-sized Tepee Lake at the channel's south end, and there saw two canoes coming lickety-split in our direction, the paddlers under a full head of steam. The canoes rocked from side to side with the power of the strokes, water rising in a V from the bows and racing to the sterns just below the gunnels.

"Mornin'!" the bowman in the first canoe called as we drew close. There were four of them, big guys in their early twenties, T-shirts, shorts and sunglasses.

"Did you pass many canoes going this way?" he said as we

drew abreast.

"None," I said.

In the centre of the lead canoe on the forward side of the thwart sat a large green cooler tied shut with a leather strap. Packed around it was a ton of gear.

"See any empty sites?"

Both canoes now past us, I had to talk over my shoulder.

"None in the channel, but we just left a site on the island on Thomson."

"Thanks."

Party-time weekenders are easy to spot. Their objective is to find a site no more than a half-day paddle from the parking lot, set up and relax, preferably with some of the good stuff I suspected the green cooler contained.

"Dad, what's that place?"

"It's Camp Arowhon, a kids' camp. Maybe all those campers we saw yesterday at the portage are staying there."

I ruddered to the right so we could have a closer look at the place.

"It looks different."

"You're thinking of Arowhon Pines, the lodge. It's a different place. We passed it on the second day over that way," I said, pointing ahead.

Arowhon was the first co-ed camp in Algonquin, opening in 1934 on Tepee Lake, just north of Canoe Lake. Its name is taken from Samuel Butler's 1872 utopian novel *Erewhon*. The Arowhon Pines Lodge opened five years later. There are other camps in the park. Ahmek, the Ojibwa name for beaver, is a boys' camp founded in 1921. Among the principles it promotes is a rich camp culture centred on values, tradition and a strong understanding of the natural environment. Tanamakoon, meaning hail-fellow-well-met, is a girls' camp that opened its cabin doors for the first time four years after Ahmek. It identifies itself as a place where "growth and fun walk hand in hand." The aims of the Tanamakoon campers are spelled out in a camp verse and include showing sincere care for all people, being disciplined in all they do and working for a peaceful world.

Another important organization, which is not a camp, was established in 1983 by a group of people who were passionate about the park. The Friends of Algonquin Park is a non-profit registered charity. Its mission is dedicated to furthering Algonquin Park's educational and interpretive programs, and for a modest fee, you and your family can become members. It has a great website.

Camp Arowhon stretched along the shore, a collection of red-roofed wooden cabins with a large log building at their centre. A dozen small sailboats were out, each with its three-girl crew practising manoeuvres. Sails flapping, the boats criss-crossed in front of each other, the girls shrieking whenever a collision looked imminent.

Riffled by the breeze, the east arm of Joe Lake sparkled in the sunlight like a field of diamonds.

"Do you know where you are?"

Suzanne shook her head.

"We camped right over there the first night, near where that log is sticking out of the water."

I aimed the paddle blade in the general direction.

"Are we going there?"

"No, we go this way. In a few minutes you'll see the bridge we went under. Remember it?"

"That's where the lady gave me the candy."

"Right. Just past it, at the dam."

I raised the binoculars and focused on the water ahead. It filled the lenses with a sheet of concentrated white fire, stabbing my eyes and reducing objects in the field of vision to silhouettes. We had closed the circle. Once past Joe Island, now in front of us, we would be retracing our outbound route.

In one way, I felt a sense of relief. Suzanne had come through safe and sound. My worry about her fainting spells and seizures and how she would make out on a canoe trip had been for naught. In fact, she had thrived, never saying too much, but seeming to grow more comfortable and confident in her new environment as the days rolled by. She had learned canoe paddling and the importance of staying seated when afloat. She had built a campfire, helped pitch a tent and understood first-hand the reason for caching your food pack up a tree well away from the trunk. Words like *gunnel, thwart, bow* and *stern* were now part of her vocabulary. She had put her face in the water, counted growth rings on a tree, acquired a rudimentary understanding of what a map was about, and had seen that no matter which way a compass turned, the needle always pointed north. She had learned that *portage* means to carry your canoe and camping gear over a forest trail. She had chased a bear with a paddle, seen a beaver and a loon up close, been lulled to sleep by the tattoo of rain on canvas and awakened to washed blue sky and the smell of wood smoke. And she had sat with me on the shore of a lake, watching the sunset as the profound silence of the darkening forest enveloped us, and in the simple gesture of wanting me to hold her, she had reminded me of our true purpose on this earth.

One weekend toward the end of my parents' lives, I went to visit them while they were still in their own home, and saw on the dining room wall a framed quotation that I could not recall being there on previous visits. It was by the American clergyman and slavery abolitionist Henry Ward Beecher: "We never know the love of a parent till we become parents ourselves. When we first bend over the cradle of our own child, God throws back the temple door and reveals to us the sacredness and mystery of a father's and mother's love to ourselves."

My mother was not a religious person in the traditional sense, but I knew those words of Beecher's would have touched her deeply. Her children and grandchildren and great-grandchildren were the focus of her life, and invariably our talks would turn in that direction. Like her, I have found that the bumpy road of parenthood is bittersweet, and looking back over my long years as a father, I can see the passage of time as a line of winding step stones, each inscribed with its particular story about our family's journey. In the campfire circles that mark our passage through the woods and prairies and mountains of Canada, we remember our stories together. When my daughters were little and we did everything together, before their teenage years, I was too inexperienced to know that those years would number among the happiest of my adult life. I miss them. I remember clearly what was for me a seismic shift in my relationship with my children, when Suzanne entered her teens and I discovered that she had a mind of her own. She began wanting to do things outside the family unit, and I experienced the distinct feeling that my role as top dog in her life was over, that I was losing control. With her sister, Laurie, following close behind, I was entering an alien arena without armour. We would have our trials and tribulations, like most families do, but together we pulled through, and now, as I approach the tail end of my time on this earth and reflection flirts with melancholy and regrets tug at the heart, I have my grandchildren, and in their exuberance for life, age rejoices in the echo of those earlier days.

I was not to see Algonquin again for a decade, as the following year a new job would take us west of the Rockies. There would be other camping trips in other places far removed from the park, but like the wandering albatross, I knew that eventually I would find my way back, and when finally I did cruise in for a landing, it was like being reacquainted with an old friend. I've been going back every summer since.

During an Algonquin trip with some friends a few years ago, our route took us right past the Burnt Island campsite Suzanne and I had shared. I pointed it out and told them about the bear and the cans in the water. There were nods of acknowledgement, nothing more, and we paddled right on by, not missing a stroke. It is an ageless truism that what is sacred ground to one man is but passing scenery to another. What are the bonds that hold us to a place, lived in for a day and remembered for a lifetime? Certainly, a shared wilderness experience is one of them. Wilderness connects one person to another, an enchanted loom that weaves place, time, body and spirit into a common fabric of uncommon strength. In the environment of the natural world, children unconsciously explore who they are and who is important to them, and in the process, plant the seeds of a better future for themselves and the earth.

Joe Island slid past on our left, and once behind us, I could feel the first hint of the Old Lady working herself up. Not wanting to be caught by her on our last day, I would leave off visiting the cairn erected to the memory of Tom Thomson until another time. Little did I suspect that a decade would pass before I would see Algonquin Park again.

"There's the bridge," I said.

As we approached, I kept expecting a car to drive across, just to let us know we were back.

"Get ready to duck," I said.

I lay back on the stern. The canoe slid smoothly under the logs with their hanging spiderwebs. A few minutes later, I let Suzanne's end of the canoe bump the shore at the dam, then brought my end around for a parallel landing to avoid getting out in deep water. For the moment, there was nobody else around. We unloaded and hauled everything to the base of a nearby tree.

"Let's sit over there on the grass for a bit and rest. This is just a short portage. It'll only take us a few minutes to get everything through."

"Is this the last portage?" she asked.

"The last one. Then one more lake to paddle and we'll be back at the restaurant. Are you getting hungry?"

She nodded, no doubt imagining the chocolate milkshake and cheeseburger in front of her.

I wasn't tired, but the water on the south side of the dam, with its motorboats and cottages, marked the end of the trip for me, and I just wanted a few final moments here in the quiet. We sat ourselves down in the same spot where we had eaten our lunch on the first day. I tamped tobacco into my pipe for the last time until the next trip, the smoke rising in a blue cloud and drifting off. Suzanne wrapped her arms around her knees, looking back the way we had come. Yellow butterflies flitted among the buttercups, and behind us the breeze whispered through the trees.

12

Algonquin Park is a place where everywhere you turn, there will always be a friend.

– Words on a cabin wall

The following account of our canoe trip was written by Suzanne in red ink on three-hole lined paper, probably for a school assignment. I found it twenty-eight years later in a cardboard box containing her and her sister's school memorabilia. I've typed it verbatim, including the strikeouts she made to correct mistakes. Since that day, she has gone on to earn two university degrees and is currently enjoying a global teaching career. Her writing has improved.

~~Algoequin~~

ALGONQuiN

One morning my dad and I ~~went~~ got a canoe and paddled of to AlgonQuin park and ~~when~~ when we got there my dad and I looked for a ~~camp~~ camping spot. Then my dad got out his bathing suit and so did I and my dad showed me how to swim and how the board float it was fun! Once my dad took my out to ~~learn~~ teach ~~learn~~ how to paddle the boat we ~~wento~~ went out all awayaround the island then it started to rain when we got back it was sunny. ~~We~~ went to bed that night and next morning we wentout rowing and when we got back we saw that some animal juring the night had got into our food. We found it was a ~~baer~~ bear and then we put out a matirealed bag and put it on a rope over the water and went to bed next morning I heard something ~~roli~~ rolling down a hill. My dad and I found out it was a bear and it got into all are food even our tang and chocolates when I got backhome I told my mum and sister.

The EnD

AFTERWORD

The first draft of this book was written in 1993, two decades after the trip. My memory of that week was still pretty good back then, and knowing Algonquin Park like I did, I think that I managed to tell the story more or less as it happened, the bear episodes in particular. An exception was our blue canoe. It was actually purchased in British Columbia in 1976, but as it served our family faithfully for the next twenty-five years, I decided to honour the happy memories it had given us and invoke poetic licence by backing up just a bit and making it our mode of travel rather than the equally heavy aluminum rental we used for that memorable Algonquin week.

Another twenty plus years and numerous canoe trips would go by before I began seriously to consider the manuscript's publication. During that long hiatus, I kept in mind my views about children and the outdoors, and in my reading, started looking for supporting sources. What surprised me was not the finding of those sources but the discovery that there were so many. I owe them a debt of thanks and have quoted some of them in this book — poets, writers, scientists, philosophers, politicians and educators. Their convictions about the importance of the natural world in our lives gave me the push I needed to get cracking and start overhauling the yellowing pages I'd typed in middle age. For further insight into the value of this book's theme, I can't do better than to direct the reader to Richard Louv's book *Last Child in the Woods: Saving Our Children from Nature-Deficit Disorder*, first published in 2005. I learned about *Last Child in the Woods* while finishing the second draft of this book, and I was delighted to see my own thoughts so thoroughly validated. It's a book every parent should read. Extensive coverage of Louv and his research, including a panel discussion with Canadian geneticist and environmental activist David Suzuki, is also available on YouTube.

I still canoe Algonquin Park. Its southernmost border is less than a half day's drive from my home. Portages are another matter. As I grow older, they get longer. I depend on the younger generations to carry the load as I once did for them, and in the spirit of the voyageurs, to keep alive the song of the paddle in the years ahead. I won't be in the boat, but I know I'll always travel with them.

I never did get the cedarstip-and-canvas Chestnut Prospector. When the blue finally became just too heavy to carry over long hauls, I wimped out and opted for a red carbon-Kevlar model at nearly half the weight. But it does have mahogany gunnels, and like Lloyd, I oil them spring and fall. They're still in good condition, but the hull has suffered a thousand scrapes on as many rocks from one side of Algonquin to the other.

When I told my cousin Marion Kennedy, a freelance editor, not to let family ties influence her edit of my second draft, she took me at my word and really put me to work. She is a big part of the final manuscript, always following up her recommended revisions with reasons for me to consider. I owe her a big thank you. Any deviation from correct spelling, punctuation, grammar and what is considered proper use of the English language is entirely my doing.

My thanks to the Ontario Ministry of Natural Resources and Forestry for its help in verifying park statistics, and special thanks to David LeGros for emailing me the 1974 edition of the park's canoe route map. It was likely a reissue of the one I had used in 1973. Reviewing its dated graphics was a nostalgic step back in time.

To Steve and Barb Whalen and their extended family, thank you for inviting me to share your Algonquin Park adventures. We took our first trip together to Big Crow Lake in 1990, and thereafter never missed a year for the next two decades. The Barron River Canyon, a capsize in fierce winds on Big Trout Lake and cliff jumping at Cork are among the memories we share. It has been my privilege to travel in your company.

To my wife, Bev, who read the manuscript numerous times and corrected me on certain points of family history, thank you for your constant support and your belief in the value of the book's theme and your encouragement to see the manuscript through to publication. We've shared the same canoe for over half a century and we're still afloat.

CPSIA information can be obtained
at www.ICGtesting.com
Printed in the USA
LVHW09s1417230818
587233LV00008B/1/P